Any work by Mike and Rubel is a welcomed event. This book promises to be one of their best!"

—Max Lucado, Best-selling Author

"If you are serious about the business of developing Christlikeness in your life, you need to read this book."

—Rick Warren, Saddleback Valley Community Church
Mission Viejo, California

"Simple yet profound—not just another 'how to' book, but a clear portrayal of the ways of our Master. Reading this book brings you face to face with the life of Jesus. I recommend it to all who would follow him."

—Randy Pope, Pastor, Perimeter Church, Duluth, Georgia

"The authors tuck the reader deep in the pleats and folds of Jesus' garments and follow him everywhere. It is a trip you won't want to miss in Bible-nourished, hyperactive space, in how to become available for life in the twenty-first century."

—Leonard I. Sweet, Author, FaithQuakes

"Mike Cope has distinguished himself as a pastor and now as a writer. I would highly recommend to anyone his unique insights in bringing Jesus' radical first-century Christianity into our own needy twentieth-century context."

—Robert M. Lewis, Teaching Pastor, Fellowship Bible Church,
Little Rock, Arkansas

"I loved it! Shelly and Cope have identified the greatest challenge before the American church: to equip the followers of Jesus Christ to live their faith in real life. The book is practical, truthful—without being judgmental!—and inspiring. If there is an application of the Gospel in contemporary America that isn't addressed in this book, I don't know what it is."

—Michael W. Foss, Prince of Peace Lutheran Church,
Burnsville, Minnesota

"Finally! Shelly and Cope have written the book I've been searching for: a book I can use with Christians to help them take the next step down the road of faithful discipleship."

—Dr. George Cladis, Pastor, Covenant Presbyterian Church,
Austin, Texas

"I need guidance for following Christ in an era that constantly takes me outside my comfort zone. This book helps me and will help many others navigate the times through the eyes and spirit of Jesus."

—Gene Appel, Senior Minister, Central Christian Church,
Las Vegas, Neveda

What
Would
Jesus
Do
Today?

What Would Jesus Do Today?

POVERTY

COMPETITION

HONESTY

COMMITMENT

STRESS

THE WORLD

MONEY

SEXUALITY

CONFUSION

INJUSTICE

RELIGION

DEATH

MIKE COPE
RUBEL SHELLY

HOWARD
PUBLISHING CO.
West Monroe, Louisiana

Our purpose at Howard Publishing is to:

- *Increase faith* in the hearts of growing Christians
- *Inspire holiness* in the lives of believers
- *Instill hope* in the hearts of struggling people everywhere

Because He's coming again!

What Would Jesus Do Today?
© 1998 Howard Publishing Co., Inc.
All rights reserved. Printed in the United States of America

Published by Howard Publishing Co., Inc.
3117 North 7th Street, West Monroe, Louisiana 71291-2227

98 99 00 01 02 03 04 05 06   10 9 8 7 6 5 4 3

Library of Congress Cataloging-in-Publication Data
Cope, Mike.
    What Would Jesus Do Today? / Mike Cope, Rubel Shelly.
       p. cm.
    Includes bibliographical references.
    ISBN 13: 978-1-4165-9796-4
    1. Christian life. 2. Jesus Christ—Person and offices.
I. Shelly, Rubel. II. Title.
BV4501.2.C67745 1998
248.4—dc21   97-41368
                                                            CIP

Jacket design by LinDee Loveland
Manuscript editing by Dr. Larry Keefauver

Scripture quotations not otherwise marked are from the New International Version (NIV), © 1973, 1978, 1984 by International Bible Society. Used by permission of Zondervan Bible Publishers. Scripture taken from *THE MESSAGE.* Copyright © 1993, 1994, 1995, 1996. Used by permission of NavPress Publishing Group.

"Magna Charta of Trust" (Leonard I. Sweet), Sweet's SoulCafe (March 1996). Used by permission.

C O N T E N T S

Come, take up your cross and follow me.

Jesus, Mark 10:21

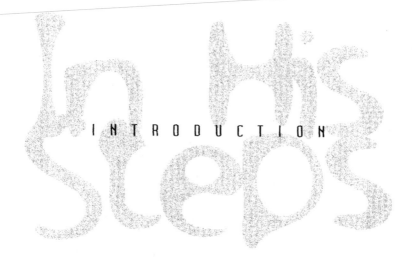

In His Steps

Several years ago, James Dobson received a letter about a three-year-old theologian named Christine and her five-year-old brother, Matthew.

Matthew had pulled the chocolate milk out of the fridge, only to discover how very little was left.

"Mom, I'm going to have to drink this by myself because there isn't enough for me *and* Christine," he said.

His dad quickly and sternly asked, "Matthew, if Jesus were here, what would he do?"

Without missing a beat, little Christine responded, "He'd make more chocolate milk!"

Sometimes big theologians come in small packages!

This humorous anecdote underscores two very important assumptions in this book:

1. The church should continue to ask what Jesus would do today.
2. The church should be familiar enough with Jesus of Nazareth as revealed in Scripture to have some idea how to answer.

The essence of Christian discipleship is *following Jesus.* Boil down all the theological explanations for how we should live, and one truth remains: *We follow Jesus Christ.* Disciples seek to understand and emulate his values, his behavior, and his view of reality. The words of Jesus after washing the disciples' feet have broad application for us:

> You call me "Teacher" and "Lord," and rightly so, for that is what I am. Now that I, your Lord and Teacher, have washed your feet, you also should wash one another's feet. I have set you an example that you should do as I have done for you. I tell you the truth, no servant is greater than his master, nor is a messenger greater than the one who sent him.[1]

When the Gospels tell us about Jesus, it isn't just for biographical insight. They are seeking to shape Christ followers more into his image. The call of Jesus, "Come, follow me," still rings out!

IN HIS STEPS

In 1896 Charles Sheldon wrote what has become one of the world's best-selling books. *In His Steps* imagines how a few people would respond when challenged one Sunday by their newly convicted minister to continually ask the question: *What would Jesus do?* This appears to be a simple question, yet it dramatically changed them, their families, their church, and their community.

Milton Jones preached a sermon in Seattle rooted in that same, simple question. At the message's conclusion, he asked the congregation if they were willing to follow Christ anywhere. To most people, Jones's challenge made perfect sense. But one man was very confused. He had made a radical conversion to Christ and had assumed that every Christian already had a deep desire to follow him. When he walked to the front of the auditorium during the invitation song, he asked Milton, "Do you mean to tell me that some of the people in this church haven't even decided whether they're going to follow Jesus or not?"

His question should echo inside every church building! Are there some who just "go to church" because of their heritage or because it is socially acceptable? Do some church members simply sit in a building Sunday after Sunday without ever committing to follow Jesus? Or have all decided that their greatest desire is to be followers of Christ?

Jesus isn't just the Savior who provided the sacrifice for our sins, as crucial as that is. He is also *Lord*, the Master whom we follow. As we read the Gospels, we must remember that not only are we recipients of Jesus' ministry, but also that we are called to continue his ministry.

Scott Peck participated in a conference for Christian therapists and counselors in which Harvey Cox told the story of when Jesus was asked to heal the daughter of a synagogue ruler named Jairus. As Christ went to Jairus's house, a woman who had been hemorrhaging for twelve years reached out to touch his robe. After asking who touched him and receiving her response, Jesus healed her and then continued to the house where the little girl had died.

After telling this powerful story from the Gospels, Cox asked six hundred "Christian professionals" with whom they most identified. When asked who connected most with the bleeding woman, about one hundred people raised their hands. A few others indicated that they identified with the anxious father. The highest number of hands were raised when Cox mentioned the curious crowd.

But when Harvey Cox asked who identified with Jesus, only six hands popped up. Scott Peck reviewed the incident and wrote about it:

> Something is very wrong here. Of six hundred more or less professional Christians, only one out of a hundred identified with Jesus. Maybe more actually did but were afraid to raise their hands lest that seem arrogant. But again something is wrong with our concept of Christianity if it seems arrogant to identify with Jesus. That is exactly what we are supposed to do! *We're supposed to identify with Jesus, act like Jesus, be like Jesus. That is what Christianity is supposed to be about—the imitation of Christ.*[2]

THREE BARRIERS

While we believe the church should once again focus on the question *What would Jesus do today?* we recognize that it faces some formidable barriers in asking the question. What are some of the problems we face in following Jesus?

1. DISTANCE

First, there is the problem of distance—many centuries separate us from Jesus' era. Not all questions the twenty-first-century church will want to address are directly answered by reading the Gospels. For example:

- How would Jesus handle the flood of images from the media?
- What use would Christ make of the Internet and telecommunications?
- How would he answer the prickly issues of homosexuality and abortion?
- What limits would Christ place on his lifestyle in this "you-are-what-you-own" culture?

Though not all modern questions can be directly and easily answered with a book, chapter, and verse from Scripture, we are surely helped by understanding Jesus in his culture. His insights into reality are timeless and true. His values then would surely be his values now.

In our efforts to overcome this barrier, we must be careful not to baptize Jesus into our culture, as so often happens. Jesus would then become (in our imagination) the kinder, gentler CEO, the encouraging coach, or the Republican (or Democrat, depending on your bent) activist.

The barrier of time demands that we study the Gospels carefully, listening to their four distinctive voices. They were given to us not so we could reconstruct our own "life of Jesus," but so we might hear their interpretations and applications of his life for the church today.

2. DISCIPLINE

A second barrier we face when posed with the question *What would Jesus do today?* involves discipline. In his insightful book *The Spirit of the Disciplines,* Dallas Willard points to a basic flaw in Sheldon's classic:

> The book does not state that to follow in [Jesus'] steps is to adapt the total manner of life he did. So the idea conveyed is an absolutely fatal one—that to follow him simply means to try to behave as he did when he was "on the spot," under pressure or persecution or in the spotlight. There is no realization that what he did in such cases was, in a large and essential measure, the natural outflow of the life he lived when not on the spot.[3]

Asking ourselves *What would Jesus do?* is the right question, but it isn't enough. To follow Jesus in moment-by-moment decisions, we must be willing to follow him continually in the practice of spiritual communion with God. We must be willing to engage in spiritual disciplines like prayer, silence, and Scripture reading. In other words, we can't live like the world 99 percent of the time and make decisions like Jesus the other 1 percent.

3. DIFFICULTY

The sheer difficulty of following Jesus is the third barrier we as Christians face. Attending church requires very little sacrifice (at least most Sundays!). Going to a class, becoming part of a church committee, and attending a special conference—these aren't exactly marathon performances!

But following Jesus? That's quite different! As G. K. Chesterton put it, "Christianity has not so much been tried and found wanting, as it has been found difficult and left untried." It's much easier to bring Jesus into one of our churches, dress him up, and tone him down than it is to encounter the Jesus of the Gospels and seek to follow him.

No wonder Christ often warned people to sit down and count the cost before jumping in behind him:

> As they were walking along the road, a man said to [Jesus], "I will follow you wherever you go." Jesus replied, "Foxes have holes and birds of the air have nests, but the Son of Man has no place to lay his head." He said to another man, "Follow me." But the man replied, "Lord, first let me go and bury my father." Jesus said to him, "Let the dead bury their own dead, but you go and proclaim the kingdom of God." Still another said, "I will follow you, Lord; but first let me go back and say good-by to my family." Jesus replied, "No one who puts his hand to the plow and looks back is fit for service in the kingdom of God."[4]

Do we really want to be Christ followers if it means changing our relationship with money or if it means loving people we consider untouchable? What if it means stepping across carefully drawn lines of class or race? And ultimately, what if it means that we have to die to ourselves?

A SECOND TOUCH

A fitting story as we launch our discovery together in this book is the healing of the blind man in Mark 8:22–26. This may be the New Testament's strangest miracle. Usually when Jesus healed a person, the healing was immediate and complete. But in this instance, his healing came in stages. After the man was touched by Jesus, his vision went from 0 to 20/200 (or so). Then when the man first saw people, they looked like trees.

In this sense, the blind man was just like the people surrounding Jesus. Their lives had been touched by him, but their vision of who he was and what it meant to follow him was fuzzy. "Do you not see?" Jesus had asked them. "Do you have eyes but fail to see? . . . Do you still not understand?"[5]

These would-be followers needed just what the (formerly) blind man needed and just what we need—a second touch from Jesus. They needed to see more clearly who this Christ was and what the cost would be if they decided to follow him.

Some of us may not want a clearer vision. We are comfortable with where we are and what we can already see. Anything more would be disorienting.

Many are like Virgil, a man whom neurologist Oliver Sacks describes in his book *An Anthropologist on Mars*. Virgil had lived a fairly contented life as a blind person. He worked as a massage therapist at a YMCA and lived in a small house the YMCA provided. He had friends, read Braille papers and books, and followed baseball carefully.

His contented life was destroyed when, at the insistence of his fiancée, he underwent a surgery that enabled him to see. While those of us who see imagine such a surgery to be a blessing of modern technology, to Virgil it was "a miracle that misfired, a calamity." Sight completely disoriented his world, demanding a radical transformation in psychological functioning, in self, and in his identity. As Dr. Sacks described it, Virgil's problem was that "one must die as a blind person to be born again as a seeing person."[6] An infant begins learning in a visual-spatial world, but a newly sighted adult is plopped down into a world in which everything contradicts an entire lifetime's experience.

In Virgil's case, his only release from the curse of sight came from a disease that returned him to blindness—a blindness he received as a gift!

Could it be that you have become contented with 20/200 vision—with a few prayers and church services and just enough Christian symbols to allow you to live like the rest of the people in the world while feeling holy?

Leonard Sweet, in his "Magna Charta of Trust by an Out-of-Control Disciple," challenges us to greater heights:

> I am part of the Church of the Out-of-Control. I once was a control junkie, but now am an Out-of-Control Disciple. I've given up my control to God. I trust and obey the Spirit. I've jumped off the fence, I've stepped over the line, I've pulled out all the stops. There's no turning back, looking around, slowing down, backing away, letting up, or shutting up. It's life Against the Odds, Outside the Box, Over the Wall, the game of life played Without Goal Lines other than "Thy will be done. . . ."
>
> I am not here to please the dominant culture. I live to please my Lord and Savior. My spiritual taste-buds have graduated from fizz to froth to Fire and Ice. Sometimes I'm called to sharpen the cutting edge, and sometimes to blunt the cutting edge. Don't give me that old-time religion. Don't give me that new-time religion. Give me that all-time religion that's as hard as rock and as soft as snow.
>
> I've stopped trying to make life work, and started trying to make life sing. I am finished with second-hand sensa-

tions, third-rate dreams, low-risk high-rise trades and goose-stepping, flag-waving crusades. I no longer live by and for anything but everything God-breathed, Christ-centered, and Spirit-driven.

I can't be bought by any personalities or perks, positions or prizes. I won't give up, though I may give in . . . to openness of mind, humbleness of heart, and generosity of spirit. In the face of adversity no longer will I hang in there. I will stand in there, I will run in there, I will pray in there, I will sacrifice in there, I will endure in there—in fact I will do everything in there but hang. My face is upward, my feet are forward, my eyes are focused, my way is cloudy, my knees are worn, my seat uncreased, my heart burdened, my spirit light, my road narrow, my mission wide.

I won't be seduced by popularity, traduced by criticism, travestied by hypocrisy or trivialized by mediocrity. I am organized religion's best friend and worst nightmare. I won't back down, slow down, shut down, or let down until I'm preached out, teached out, healed out or hauled out of God's mission in the world entrusted to members of the Church of the Out-of-Control . . . to unbind the confined, whether they're the downtrodden or the upscale, the overlooked or the underrepresented.

My fundamental identity is as a disciple of Jesus—but even more, as a disciple of Jesus who lives in Christ, who doesn't walk through history simply "in his steps," but seeks to travel more deeply *in his Spirit.*

Until he comes again or calls me home, you can find me filling not killing time so that one day he will pick me out in the lineup of the ages as one of his own. And then . . . it will be worth it all . . . to hear these words, the most precious words I can ever hear:

"Well done, thou good and faithful . . . Out-of-Control Disciple."[7]

Are you out of control and loving it? Would you be willing to be touched again by Jesus in order to see more clearly who he is and what it means to follow him?

As you walk through this book, ask anew the old question—What would Jesus do today?

The phrase "the worldly church" could have either negative or positive connotations. It could mean the church has sold out to the values of the culture around it and has lost its counter-culture message. . . . The church can simply become a reflection of the world. This, of course, is sinful and disastrous.

But it could also mean the church has been willing to do its work outside the camp where Jesus [is], and this is faithfulness to our calling. If you have been mounted on the wall defending the fortress, aren't you ready for a new kind of ministry, the ministry of the trenches, the ministry of woe and misery, the ministry of disgrace, the ministry of Jesus?

Randy Harris, *Wineskins Magazine*

CHAPTER ONE

The World

By watching and listening to some Christians, we might think Jesus said, "You are the scud missiles of the world." Many of these Christians advocate that we should treat the world (including people whose lives aren't exemplary) as the enemy.

- They wage battles and condemn.
- They declare culture war and launch deadly verbal missiles.
- They leap into politics and fire charges, caring little about accuracy.

By their lopsided response, they express God's judgment without his compassion.

On the other hand, some Christians live as if Jesus said, "You are the frosting of the earth." They think and act as if there were only minimal differences between Christians and the world.

- They ignore significant issues.
- They make neutrality and tolerance a litmus test of faithfulness.
- They blend in like chameleons.

Such responses express God's compassion without his judgment and justice.

For centuries Christ followers have been trying to figure out how to live in a fallen, sinful world. This search has led some to escape into tiny Christian subcultures where they could feel "holy," and it has led others to conform to world appearances and become comfortable by adopting the world-view and values of the unredeemed.

Such compromising Christians walk as close to the edge of the great divide between the world and the Word as they can while hoping not to fall over the edge. They vainly attempt to juggle worldly values while walking a spiritual tightrope. The bottom line is that the world has no safety net, and too many Christians find themselves falling back into world crevasses, even though they have ostensibly given their lives to Christ.

The only accurate guide to living is Jesus Christ himself. He is the embodiment of both God's righteousness and compassion.

WHAT JESUS TAUGHT

Christ's teachings are direct and to the point! Using two simple, powerful metaphors, Jesus explained our relationship with those around us who aren't Christ followers:

- You are the *salt* of the earth. But if the salt loses its saltiness, how can it be made salty again? It is no longer good for anything, except to be thrown out and trampled by men.

- You are the *light* of the world. A city on a hill cannot be hidden. Neither do people light a lamp and put it under a bowl. Instead they put it on its stand, and it gives light to everyone in the house. In the same way, let your light shine before men, that they may see your good deeds and praise your Father in heaven.[1]

I've often wondered if anyone laughed when Jesus taught this! These weren't, after all, the powerbrokers of Rome or the philosophical elite of Athens or the exporters of Alexandria. These people were Galilean and Judean peasants. Nonetheless, Jesus had chosen to perform God's mighty works among them! They were the poor in spirit, the mourners, the meek, the hungry and thirsty, the merciful, the pure in heart, the peacemakers, and the persecuted.[2] They were broken people who had nowhere to go but to the open arms of God.

These righteousness-seeking, peace-building, word-honoring people created a revival that God used to speak to the world. By their transformed lives, others would be directed to their "Father in heaven."[3]

A few years ago, a man wrote to the *New York Times* about a transformation he had witnessed in Damascus, Syria. He had seen a bicyclist cycling while balancing a crate of oranges on his handlebars. Making his way toward the cyclist was another man carrying a heavy parcel. The two collided, and oranges began rolling down the street. A nuclear war of words broke out. The battle escalated when the orange owner raised his clenched first. Suddenly, out of the crowd that had gathered, a small man appeared, grabbed the fist, kissed it, and disappeared. Disarmament and peace soon followed. Instead of two brawling men and a cheering crowd, there were two relaxed men and a crowd trying to reclaim all the oranges. Peacemakers. Mercy lovers. Spiritual seekers. These are the ones whom Jesus said would have the great impact on the world.

Of course the metaphors aren't particularly complimentary to the world. The fact that it needs salt implies that it is rotting. Why? Because salt was used during that time to stop the putrefaction process. And the need for light points to the world's darkness. Despite thinking of itself as enlightened and modern, this world is in the dark. Darkness can no more provide light for itself than rotting meat can preserve itself.

It isn't our job to express shock at the world, but to be salt and light in the world. I am continually amazed when I hear Christians express their shock at how dark the world is. They are shocked by the language people use, by what's on television, and by legislation that is introduced in some state legislatures. But why should this surprise us? By calling us the salt and light, Jesus implied that the world is in great need.

These two word pictures imply two very important principles for us as we seek to live as Jesus would live.

1. We must not be identical. When salt is diluted with sand, it becomes useless as a preservative.

- What happens when Christians are as consumed with materialism as the world?
- What about when they are as shady as the world in the way they turn business deals?
- When Christians mistreat their spouses or dishonor their marriage vows, how are they salt and light in the world?
- What help is there for the world when Christians parade their pompous power or seek success as defined in the media?
- What light is there when we have the same heroes and the same eagerness for revenge and when we engage in the same backbiting as the world?

To be the salt of the gospel, we must not be mixed with the sand of unrighteousness. We must seek a righteousness that "surpasses that of the Pharisees and the teachers of the law."[4]

Even though a Christian man works in the same office building as the worldly man, there must be something different about him. He refuses to participate in lustful, demeaning comments about women. He avoids treating money as if it can give him meaning, prestige, or life. He works hard to live out the vows he made to his wife. He doesn't hold grudges, and he doesn't play meaningless games in order to succeed.

Even though a Christian teenager goes to the same school and has the same friends, she is different from her peers. She likes to look nice but has learned that her value as a person doesn't come from how she looks or from designer clothing labels. She enjoys romance but is committed to being sexually pure. In many ways she's "normal," but still—there's something very different about her!

2. We must not be isolated. As the children's song instructs us, "Hide it under a bushel? *No!*" (screamed at decibel levels that would offend a rock band!). However, many Christians seem to believe that the goal is to get away from the world. If they could just live around other Christians, socialize, vacation, and keep their children around other Christians' children, then everything would be great.

That was the approach of the Qumran community during the time Jesus lived. Calling themselves "children of light," they wanted to escape from the "sons of darkness" (meaning just about everyone but themselves). But their righteous "salt" was as useless as the deposits on the shores of the nearby Dead Sea. God doesn't intend for us to retreat to Christian subcultures!

Just before his death, Jesus prayed about his followers and their place in this world, saying:

> My prayer is not that you take them out of the world but that you protect them from the evil one. They are not of the world, even as I am not of it. Sanctify them by the truth; your word is truth. As you sent me into the world, I have sent them into the world.[5]

We who seek to follow Jesus Christ have been called to be in the world, but not of the world. We are salt not scud missiles; light not frosting. We are neither to conform to the sinful practices and ungodly values of this world nor to retreat from the people of this world who are caught up in such practices and values. And our model in seeking this "in-but-not-of" balance is Jesus Christ. Note that Jesus prayed, "As you sent me into the world, I have sent them into the world."

How Jesus Lived

The vivid "visual aid" Jesus provided with his life didn't slip past the notice of the writer of Hebrews. "We do not have a high priest who is unable to sympathize with our weaknesses, but we have one who has been tempted in every way, just as we are—yet was without sin."[6]

It was scandalously clear that Jesus did not try to isolate himself from the world. The fact that he came as God *in flesh* is remarkable. God did not choose to treat this world with antiseptic spray and rubber gloves. Rather, he came to live among us. What greater call to live among lost people could there be than this?

Not only did he become a man, but Jesus also lived among men and women—many of whom weren't exactly "morally spit-shined." Christ's harshest critics, whose halos were a bit too tight to tolerate the "unholiness" of Jesus, complained about his behavior. They protested that "the Son of Man came eating and drinking" and that he was "a glutton and a drunkard, a friend of tax collectors and 'sinners.'"[7] Apparently, they would have preferred that God's incarnation hang around the temple twenty-four hours a day teaching and praying. But to be at parties? To be with tax collectors and prostitutes? Scandalous!

A Pharisee named Simon invited Jesus to his house for dinner. The evening might have gone well except that a woman who "had lived a sinful life" showed up. She wept in Jesus' presence and then anointed his feet with expensive perfume, kissing and wiping them with her hair. Simon tried to give Jesus the benefit of the doubt: If Jesus really knew what kind of woman she was, he wouldn't have permitted it.[8]

But Jesus did know, and he loved her still! His life was filled with compassion, having come to seek and save those who were lost. Rather than fire verbal missiles about the moral misconduct of the woman and others like her, Jesus embodied and spoke of God's transforming love.

Clearly, Jesus did not conform to the values and behaviors of this world. That's why the writer of Hebrews added that Christ was "without sin." Though he hung around sinners, Jesus did not sin.

After his baptism, Jesus immediately faced an intense forty-day temptation by Satan.[9] At the end of forty days in the desert, Satan baited Jesus three times, hoping to reel Jesus in through compromise. He offered shortcuts to fame, promises of power, and food for praise. Yet Jesus never bit.

Even when these three great temptations were past, Jesus would still face the lure of sin. Luke says that the devil left him "until an opportune time."[10] And there were many such "opportune times" throughout Christ's ministry. Since the Hebrews writer insists that Jesus was "tempted in every way, just as we are,"[11] we may correctly assume that Jesus was tempted by the pull of worldly success, the glitter and live-for-today thrill of materialism, and the tug of sexual impulses. Yet time after time he rejected temptation and chose the route of holiness.

Jesus was an expert at what John Stott has called "double listening." He listened to (and obeyed) the voice of God in Scripture. And he listened to the voices of men and women around him discerning their deepest needs while refusing to be trapped by their enticements to sin. Choosing to be holy, Jesus lived in the world while still separating himself from the world's sin.

HOLY IN THE WORLD

As Christians wanting to live as Jesus would, we must remember the words of an old song, "This World Is Not My Home." We live, work, play, and raise families here in this world.

But we don't exactly belong here. That's why early Christian writers would refer to the people of faith as "aliens."

> All these people were still living by faith when they died. They did not receive the things promised; they only saw them and welcomed them from a distance. And they admitted that they were aliens and strangers on earth. People who say such things show that they are looking for a country of their own.[12]

> Dear friends, I urge you, as aliens and strangers in the world, to abstain from sinful desires, which war against your soul. Live such good lives among the pagans that, though they accuse you of doing wrong, they may see your good deeds and glorify God on the day he visits.[13]

That is also why the apostle Paul would point out that since our lives have been redefined by the life, death, and resurrection of Christ and since we are now waiting for him to return, "our citizenship is in heaven."[14]

The most powerful thing the people of God can do in this world is to live as the people of God! God has placed us in communities of faith where the faith, hope, and love of the gospel can be lived out.

Admittedly, this "plan" has always been less than satisfying. Many seem to long for the "good old days" of the fourth century when Constantine declared Christianity to be the state religion. The truth is that Christianity always thrives best as a minority and becomes anemic when it is declared a majority. We are healthiest when we live out kingdom values in the midst of ungodliness. The more quasi-Christian a nation becomes, the less vibrant the church's health becomes!

A dangerous trend among believers today is the attempt to "return this nation to God." The prevailing illusion is that this was at one time a Christian nation. But Christ followers have no ultimate allegiance to one country. We are loyal patriots wherever we live. Ugandan Christians are loyal to the country of Uganda just as Brazilian Christians are loyal to Brazil. And U.S. Christians are loyal to the United States. But whether any one of these countries thrives or falls doesn't ultimately affect us, for our hope is in God's kingdom.

Sincere attempts to "return America to God" are as wrong-headed as it would have been for the church in Ephesus to start a "return Rome to God" campaign. That wasn't the model Jesus set out for them. Christ wasn't interested in "traditional Roman values" or "traditional American values." He was interested in the kingdom that had broken through in his glorious ministry. He didn't station Peter in Rome to give a daily update on what the Roman Senate was doing. Rather, he sent Peter (and the other disciples) to city after city to proclaim that the kingdom had arrived.

We are called by Christ to live out the truth of the gospel in the midst of this world. Rather than scold the world as we weep and wail over the godlessness around us, we should pray for the people of our world, live holy lives among them, and gently point them to the Father.

We are not of this world. We cannot conform to its thinking and living. John's warnings about "the world" referred to sinful attitudes and behaviors—not to people:

> Do not love the world or anything in the world. If anyone loves the world, the love of the Father is not in him. For everything in the world—the cravings of sinful man, the lust of his eyes and the boasting of what he has and does—comes not from the Father but from the world. The world and its desires pass away, but the man who does the will of God lives forever.[15]

In a culture where some kill themselves over *things*, we are content with whatever we have, because God is our true source of life. In an environment where marriages are kept as long as they're convenient, we commit ourselves to a covenant between two people. Amidst a cacophony of raging voices, we trumpet the singular note of forgiveness. In a world where racism is rearing its ugly mug again, we announce that Jesus loved all the little children of the world. We are the lights of the world!

We must not be "of the world" if we are to follow Jesus. Our lives must be distinctive. But we also must be "in the world." Rather than escape, hide, build high walls, and then pull up the draw bridge, we must open ourselves to men and women who are lost in every sense of the word.

When Paul wrote to the church in Corinth about dealing with an immoral person, he made sure they understood he wasn't talking about immoral people in the world: "I have written you in my letter not to associate with sexually immoral people—not at all meaning the people of this world who are immoral, or the greedy and swindlers, or idolaters. In that case you would have to leave the world."[16]

And as a follower of the one who was accused of being a glutton and drunkard, Paul obviously does not want us to isolate ourselves from people in the world. He expects us to be involved in the lives of people who are greedy and promiscuous, who can't be trusted, who dishonor marriage, and whose language is peppered with four-letter words. What these people need aren't "traditional American values." They need God, and their initial contact with God will be through flesh-and-blood believers.

Sheldon Vanauken wrote in his classic *A Severe Mercy* that in his struggle for faith the strongest argument for Christianity had been the joy, certainty, and completeness he saw in some believers.[17] We are fully engaged in the world because Jesus was.

Let's look at a couple of issues that are becoming more accepted and less disputed in our society: abortion and homosexuality.

Many Christians are appropriately concerned about the large number of abortions in the United States and the escalating acceptance of homosexuality. Several members in my congregation have asked me what our church is going to do about these problems. Do we have a plan? Absolutely! But our plan isn't the one that seems to be practiced so often today. We aren't going to express shock that anyone could disagree with us. (I'm going to assume that people who don't follow Jesus Christ would quite often not share my values.) We refuse to demonize homosexuals and those who have abortions. And we will not invest our primary energy in enacting legislation.

What will we do? We will continue to live as God's people in the midst of a fallen world! We will continue to believe that the greatest realities are unseen. We will continue to live knowing that the future has already broken through in the ministry of Christ and his Spirit.

As Christ followers, what are we going to do about abortion?

- Because of our allegiance to Jesus Christ as the risen Lord, we will call on our members to have sex only in marriage. While we aren't amazed that others are promiscuous, we hope that in our lives they'll see something sane and meaningful and ask about it.

- We'll continue to call for the protection of all those who are weak and have little voice: the poor, the disabled, the retarded, the broken, the unborn.

- When a child is conceived out of wedlock, we'll make sure that there is an option for the mother. We won't just march in front of a clinic to condemn her. Rather, we'll offer her love and the support and alternatives she needs to let the baby live.

- And when someone faces up to an abortion from her past (or his past since abortions often result because men are unwilling to own up to the consequences of their actions), we will be a community where confession can be made and the forgiveness of God can be stated and celebrated.

As Christ followers, how will we respond to homosexuality?

- Our response to homosexuality follows the same course as our response to abortion. The church should be ashamed of some of the hateful, demonizing rhetoric that has been fired against people whom God loves. We need to hold up both God's judgment and his compassion.

- We'll live as the people of God. We'll continue to insist that heterosexual marriage is the God-ordained place for sexual expression.

- We'll love those who struggle with their sexuality, pointing them to Jesus Christ as the only one who can fill their lives and promising to assist them in their struggle. People who struggle with homosexual temptations—including even those who are loud and belligerent about their lifestyle—are people whom God loves and desires relationship with. Our goal isn't to win battles by crushing them with our moral attacks but to be redemptive.

ENGAGED BUT NOT MARRIED

Since Jesus is our model, we are seeking to be fully engaged in the world without being married to it. We will refuse the two easy ways out: conforming to the world or escaping from the world. We'll live as reliable citizens here, but we will have citizenship in the kingdom of heaven, which has already come in Jesus Christ.

Never underestimate the significant influence of one:

- Christian nurse
- Christian high school student
- Christian teacher or coach
- Christian factory worker

- Christian parent

- Christian neighbor

We live in the place of Jesus Christ to people around us.

When we model his holiness and compassion, we reflect his light into the great darkness, and through us, those who dwell in darkness see glimpses of the Light of the World—Jesus Christ.

Can you build a fire in your lap
    and not burn your pants?
Can you walk barefoot on hot coals
    and not get blisters?
It's the same when you have sex with your
    neighbor's wife:
    Touch her and you'll pay for it. No excuses. . . .
Adultery is a brainless act,
    soul-destroying, self-destructive;
Expect a bloody nose, a black eye,
    and a reputation ruined for good.

Solomon, Proverbs 6:27–29 *THE MESSAGE*

CHAPTER TWO

Sexuality

What a thrill it was for me to run the Boston Marathon with forty thousand other runners in 1996 for the hundredth anniversary of the famed race. When the gun went off at noon on Patriot's Day, we all began making our way from Hopkinton to Boston on a two-lane road. Talk about crowded! It took runners at the end of the line more than twenty minutes just to reach the starting line. Then it was elbow-to-elbow and aching-calves-to-aching-calves for most of the race.

Now imagine what it would have been like to line up at the front of such a crowd and then to run in the opposite direction of everyone else when the gun sounded. Picture the puzzled looks, the ridicule, the bruised ribs, and the trampled toes. It might have been safer to try driving clockwise (against the traffic) in the Indy 500!

Now you have a somewhat accurate picture of what is meant by swimming against the stream. And you have a pretty good idea of what a life of sexual purity looks like today. The strong current of immorality is all around us. Swimming against the current takes more energy and strength than many have.

In many environments today, people expect sexual immorality—even with young teenagers. They merely encourage them to use precaution and protection. This public attitude was evident in the mid-1990s when a popular actor was picked up with a prostitute on Sunset Boulevard. He faced terrible public ridicule because he'd been unfaithful to his gorgeous live-in girlfriend. (Stupidity was evidently a more serious charge than sexual misconduct!) Both his actions and the public's reactions made the seventh commandment prohibiting adultery seem outdated.

Perhaps the clearest insight into the world's perspective is a question asked at the end of *The Scarlet Letter*, a 1995 film starring Demi Moore and based very loosely on Nathaniel Hawthorne's classic novel: "Who is to say what is a sin in God's eyes?" Hester Prynne lands in the twenty-first century!

It isn't really news that immorality fills television—from morning soaps to racy afternoon talk shows to prime-time sitcoms. Even the news is tainted. *USA Today* (that paragon of virtue and chastity!) reported that "the nightly newscast is chockablock with explicit language, lust, and perversion. TV moguls weep with grati tude: this carnal cornucopia has spilled into . . . their ratings sweep."

Not everyone with a television is limited to the shows that are programmed, however. Thanks to VCRs and video stores, we can be more selective about what we watch. And what are people watching? Well, there's an interesting mix as one recent top-twenty list of video sales shows. The list included:

1. *Pinocchio*
2. *Playboy Playmate of the Year*
3. *Beauty and the Beast*
4. *Playboy Celebrity Centerfold*
5. *Disney's Sing Along Songs: Friend Like Me*
8. *Playboy 1993 Video Playmate Review*
10. *Barney Rhymes with Mother Goose*
12. *101 Dalmatians*
14. *Barney's Best Manners*
15. *Playboy: Erotic Fantasies III*
18. *Playboy: The Girls of the Cabaret Royale*
19. *Penthouse: The All-Pet Workout*
20. *Barney's Magical Musical Adventure*

I'm guessing someone sent Dad to the store for a video for the kids and he grabbed one for himself while he was there. One can only hope that "Barney's Magical Musical Adventure" isn't a euphemism for some XXX-rated porno flick!

And now, thanks to the magic of telecommunications, the current of immorality can flow into our home computers. Courtesy of on-line services and the Internet, people of all ages can enter into sexual conversations (cybersex), check kinky alternative bulletin boards, and download pornography in the privacy of their own homes.

We need not be shocked that the world lives by standards no higher than enjoyment and precaution. And as the church we do not need to waste our time whining about how immoral the world is.

We mention the white rapids of this stream not to condemn the stream but to challenge those who are supposed to be swimming against it. What decisions will you, as a follower of Jesus Christ, make because of your commitment to him?

After admitting that he and his fiancée were already sexually involved, a twenty-year-old student recoiled defensively when I challenged him to refrain from continued sexual activity until they were married. For a few minutes I engaged in a debate that I was losing. Whenever I gave a reason why they should wait (e.g., "You don't know that you'll remain together"), he had a quick reply. There was just no way they were going to break up, he assured me. And there was no way that sharing a bed together could be damaging, he reasoned.

Finally, I did what I should have done initially. I asked him if he was a disciple of Jesus. When he assured me he was, I said, "Then that seems to settle it. I don't guess I understand all the reasons why Jesus doesn't want you to have sex before you're married, but then discipleship doesn't mean following Jesus only when you understand all his reasons. When you follow him, you place your trust in him. You admit that he can control your life even when it doesn't make complete sense or feel right. I want to encourage you to trust Jesus by refraining from having sex until you're married." That seemed to make more sense to him than all the other arguments combined.

I heard one man tell a small group about the time his daughter called long distance from college to ask him to explain again why she shouldn't have sex before she was married. If it had been my daughter, my first question would probably have been, "Where are you calling from?" I'd just pray she wasn't calling from a car phone!

As her father, I would hope to have the presence of mind to speak not of diseases and unwanted pregnancies but of discipleship. What would Jesus do?

WHAT JESUS TAUGHT

Perhaps the place to begin is to point out that Jesus was not antisex, as some have misunderstood him. When some Pharisees tried to pull him into the raging debate concerning divorce and remarriage, Jesus insisted that all discussion should return to God's original intentions for marriage in Genesis 2.

"Haven't you read," he asked them, "that at the beginning the Creator 'made them male and female'?"[1] Didn't they remember that God had intended for a husband and wife to become "one flesh" (a phrase that implies more than the sexual relationship, but which surely includes it)?

Jesus understood that sexuality isn't a punishment from Satan to be endured but a gift from God to be celebrated in marriage. He knew that the Creator could have devised other ways for babies to be born but chose instead to make us sexual beings.

It's important that our children grasp this truth. They will pick up on our many warnings about sexual immorality. But if we don't balance the warnings with teaching about God's delight in sexuality, they'll wind up thinking sex is evil.

Yes, sex is a good gift from God, according to Jesus. Yet it's a gift that is to be fully opened only in marriage. Jesus condemned adultery (sexual involvement by someone who's married with a person other than his or her spouse) and sexual immorality (sometimes translated "fornication"—any sexual involvement outside of marriage).

Those who follow Christ have learned to trust his guidance for sexuality. They believe that any limitations he has placed on the gift are to protect us, not to deprive us of enjoyment. They accept this heaven-sent blessing, enjoying it fully only in the context of the marriage relationship in which a man and a woman have promised to stay together. Only in marriage can sex be explored and enjoyed fully.

In God's design, two people are to remain together—no ejection seats or rip cords—whether the romantic voltage is high or low at the moment. In marriage by God's intentions, there is a commitment that transcends the hot and cold fluctuations of erotic passion.

We have a huge problem with our culture in that many of the icons considered "sexual experts" (because they engage in endless sexual explorations or endless discussions of sexual explorations) actually know very little about sex. They tend to limit sex to mere anatomy when in reality it is multidimensional.

God, the Creator of all males and females, is the only one who fully comprehends all the implications of our sexuality. He knows that there is much more to sex than what can be illustrated in a textbook! And this one who fully understands is the one who has protected us by limiting the sexual relationship to marriage.

The religious leaders of Jesus' day would certainly have agreed with him up to this point. But then he took God's intentions even deeper:

> You have heard that it was said, "Do not commit adultery." But I tell you that anyone who looks at a woman lustfully has already committed adultery with her in his heart. If your right eye causes you to sin, gouge it out and throw it away. It is better for you to lose one part of your body than for your whole body to be thrown into hell. And if your right hand causes you to sin, cut it off and throw it away. It is better for you to lose one part of your body than for your whole body to go into hell.[2]

One can be technically chaste but full of immorality, according to Jesus. When confronted by Pharisees and teachers of the law who were disturbed that his disciples didn't follow their traditions about hand washing before eating, Jesus answered that evil doesn't come from what goes into a person, but from what comes out of a person's heart. "For out of the heart come evil thoughts, murder, adultery, sexual immorality, theft, false testimony, slander. These are what make a man 'unclean'; but eating with unwashed hands does not make him 'unclean.'"[3] Sexual conduct isn't primarily about hormones; it is a matter of what is in one's heart. Therefore, a person can commit a sexual sin while fully clothed in a classroom, at a desk in the office, or in the living room of his or her own home.

Because God made all people in his image, it is wrong for us to reduce others to objects of our sexual desires. That is what Jesus calls "lust." Lust is more than looking at someone and finding them attractive or looking at them and having a sexual thought. After all, God is the one who wired us so that we can have such thoughts.

But just as appropriate anger can easily turn into bitterness, so an appropriate sexual thought can become lust. The lustful man or woman looks at another person with the intention of feeding his or her fantasies and then turns the other into little more than a sexual fantasy object. A translation that brings out Jesus' intentions would be: "Anyone who looks after a woman for the purpose of lusting after her has already committed adultery." Lust eventually becomes obsessed with fulfilling one's desires, even knowing it's against God's will.

Jesus' instruction on sexuality is concise and refreshing in an age of misinformation. Here are at least three of his insights for Christ followers:

1. Sex is a gift from a loving Creator.
2. Sexual relationships are to be confined to marriage.
3. Because all our actions are from our hearts, we must be pure in our thinking as well as in our actions.

How Jesus Lived

Jesus Christ was fully human, yet fully divine. Orthodox Christianity has always believed this despite being unable to explain it completely.

Heresy has been passed on through the centuries by those who believe one aspect of his being but not the other. Some have insisted that he was fully human but not really God—a prophet of God, perhaps, or maybe even "a son of God," adopted by the Father for his purposes. But he was not truly God.

Others have claimed that Jesus was indeed God, but that he only seemed to be human. Apparently the apostle John had to face such false teachers, for he sternly wrote: "This is how you can recognize the Spirit of God: Every spirit that acknowledges that Jesus Christ has come in the flesh is from God, but every spirit that does not acknowledge Jesus is not from God."[4]

Many Christians struggle with believing that Jesus Christ, the King of kings and Lord of lords, was fully human. They're very uncomfortable with the idea that Jesus faced sexual temptations.

Yet the writer of Hebrews claimed that he was "tempted in every way, just as we are."[5] This surely includes the sexual temptations that most men (and women) face.

But Jesus never caved in to his desires! Hebrews adds, "yet [he] was without sin." He was with many women—some emotionally vulnerable and some with sordid sexual histories. Yet he never used women as objects of his desire. Consider these examples:

1. *The woman at the well.* When Jesus met a woman from Samaria at a well, a woman who had gone through five husbands and was now living with another man, he treated her with complete respect and spoke to her about living water that wells up to eternal life.[6]

2. *The woman caught in adultery.* When a woman caught in the act of adultery was cast in front of Jesus by some religious do-gooders, Jesus got rid of the hypocrites and then spoke with great love and dignity to the poor woman, calling her to a new life in God.[7]

3. *The woman who anointed Jesus' feet.* When a woman with a sordid sexual history began wiping his feet with her tears and with perfume and then drying them with her hair, Jesus defended her to a man who was offended, insisting that her actions came as a response to God's marvelous forgiveness in her life.[8]

Jesus treated all the women he encountered as dignified individuals, pointing them back to God, who alone could make them complete. Surely there were temptations along the way (at least the writer of Hebrews was sure there were). But because Jesus' heart was eager to serve God through loving others purely, he never crossed an inappropriate line.

Doesn't it help you to know that you're following one who can sympathize with you in your temptations?

SWIMMING UPSTREAM

So how do we deal with lustful inclinations? Jesus told us to gouge out our eyes and cut off our hands if we must. This hyperbolic language certainly makes a point: *We are to take drastic measures to be sexually pure.* Don't pamper sin. Don't flirt with it. Don't nibble at sin like a fish toying with bait.

Remember that Jesus' words are not just for individuals but also for a group—a new community, the church, seeking to follow him. The church must be a group of people who . . .

- call for moral purity
- remind each other in worship of why we live differently
- confess (usually in some small group setting) our struggles and failures
- hear again and again God's word of forgiveness

One powerful Sunday at a church in Abilene, Texas, following a message on sexual purity, all high school and middle school students were dismissed to a large room. There they were met by the elders and their wives and by some of the youth leaders. They listened as these godly people committed themselves to modeling sexual purity before them and to praying for them. Then the teens were asked to raise their hands during a prayer if they would pledge themselves for a year to sexual abstinence because of God's love and because of Jesus' example of purity. In a separate room, several hundred university students met with their leaders to make similar pledges before God. Many other prayers for courage to be pure were offered by those remaining in the auditorium. We live or die as a community!

Christ followers need to encourage each other to seek good and avoid evil. They should also try to cut off the supply for whatever fuels their lust—like movies, magazines, novels, and television shows that are filled with sexual temptations. (Keep in mind that no one person has been made vice president in charge of moral limits for a church. These are personal decisions—though still made in the context of community.)

Sports Illustrated, source of the annual swimsuit edition, isn't usually a primary source for encouragement in this area. But in 1996 the cover story was about David Robinson, all-star center for the San Antonio Spurs and a dedicated Christian. The magazine spotlighted his eagerness for sexual purity:

> The Silver Dancers come onto the court during a timeout, and David Robinson does not watch. He sits at the end of the San Antonio Spurs' bench with his perfect posture, drinking a cup of water, looking down at coach Bob Hill diagramming a play. The Silver Dancers are the Spurs' version of the Laker Girls, choreographed for the maximum number of jiggles and pelvic thrusts. Their uniform tonight is hot pants and tight silver shirts. The predominant lyric in the heavy-beat music is "Do that thing." Do that thing. Do that thing. Do that thing.
>
> *Do that thing?*
>
> No, David Robinson does not watch. Assorted other Spurs, especially at the outer reaches of the huddle, can be seen sneaking peeks, uh-huh, and second looks. Last season's Most Valuable Player somehow removes himself from this part of the show. He says he never looks at the Silver Dancers. Not on purpose. He will not allow his mind to wander down the mildly carnal paths that are offered to the Alamodome crowd of 23,883. Why open himself to the possibility of impure thoughts?[9]

The article explains that the reason he will not let his eyes wander is that he is committed to following Jesus Christ. "I made a rule when I got married," he mentions when asked about all the women who try to flirt with him. "I decided that if anyone's feelings are going to be hurt, they're not going to be my wife's. If I think someone is acting inappropriately, I say so. It may sound harsh, but that's the way it is. My wife is not going to be the one to suffer."

As Christians, we must be willing to swim upstream against the world's current of prevailing immorality. Such an upstream response from one who travels in NBA circles seems heroic. But it's the same response every follower of Jesus Christ must have. While there are dozens of reasons why we want to remain pure, the main reason far surpasses all the others: because Jesus was pure!

With a swelling flood of impurity around us, we need to make firm commitments and we need to fill our hearts in such a way that we can keep those commitments. We need to set ourselves in a direction and stick with it. And Jesus has a direction for us: upstream!

Are you up to the challenge?

What is serious to us is often very trivial in the sight of God. What in God's sight might appear to us as "play" is perhaps what God . . . takes most seriously.

Thomas Merton, *New Seeds of Contemplation*

CHAPTER THREE

Stress

Americans today make more money, have more labor-saving technology, have more leisure time, and spend more on recreation than any previous generation in our country's history. Yet the most common complaint we make has to do with *having too little time* and *feeling worn out.* So after inventing gadgets to free us from monotonous tasks and taking vacations to refresh ourselves, why are we so stressed out?

The American Academy of Family Physicians says that two-thirds of all office visits to family physicians involve some stress-related symptoms. Research claims that something between 75 and 90 percent of all visits to physicians can be traced to stress. Stress is known to contribute either directly or indirectly to coronary artery disease, cancer, lung ailments, cirrhosis of the liver, accidental injuries, and suicide.

In the spring of 1996 the effects of stress on public figures came to the forefront again when the navy's top admiral took his own life. He had served two tours of duty in Vietnam, commanded ship crews, worked at the Pentagon, and served as chief of NATO's forces in Southern Europe before being promoted to the navy's top post in 1994. By all accounts he had been doing an excellent job at his post. But in the wake of sexual-harassment charges involving the navy, scandals at the Naval Academy, and criticism aimed at his leadership, the stress mounted on this soft-spoken man.

Everything came to a head for Admiral Michael Boorda as two *Newsweek* reporters were scheduled to interview him about two bronze pins for valor, called "combat Vs." He had worn them on two of the ribbons he wore on his chest to chronicle his forty years of service. Leaving for lunch prior to the meeting, he took a .38 pistol and shot himself in the chest. He left a note to "the sailors" expressing the fear that controversy over his decorations would damage the institution to which he had devoted his life. So a man who had handled much more dangerous situations became one more among the thirty thousand annual suicides in America because of the proverbial straw that broke the camel's back.

Stress can do that to people. It is less the crisis of one monumental challenge than the maddening faucet drip of accumulated frustrations. It is less the high mountain to climb than having to walk every day with a handful of pebbles in our shoes.

USA Today raised this question in an editorial following Boorda's death: "And wouldn't a ship's captain know that even the fiercest of storms end if he has the patience to weather them?"[1] Weathering storms. That's what much of life is. Illness, financial crisis, moral failure, flat tire on the way to a crucial appointment— each is a tempest that threatens to capsize your personal canoe. So how can your faith help you deal with stress?

WORRYING MOST ABOUT WHAT MATTERS LEAST

The word *stress* comes from a Latin word that means "to be drawn tight." I'll bet you know the feeling, don't you? Ever get a tight feeling through your neck and shoulders at work? What about your stomach? Or maybe you feel it in your leg muscles. Your body is responding in obvious ways to the pressures you are sensing.

Psychologists explain that our bodies respond negatively to stress by going through three successive stages: alarm, resistance, and exhaustion.

Alarm. Imagine, for example, that you are driving to work and a car suddenly cuts in front of you. Alarm is the fear of an accident or anger at the person who put you at risk. In response to it, your body dumps chemicals that may cause your face to flush, your heart rate to increase, perspiration to form, and the muscles in your arms, back, and legs to tighten.

Resistance. The next stage, resistance, allows your body to begin repairing the damage stress has caused. A calm, serene completion of your drive will allow your body to recover from the alarm response it has just made. But suppose you don't have a pleasant conclusion to the drive. Suppose instead that there is bumper-to-bumper traffic on the way to work. You stay in that same traffic flow for another half hour and get cut off three more times! Your body gets no time to recover. Your stress soon becomes distress as your body conditions you to a tense posture and attitude. So you walk into your classroom or office and snap at someone for no good reason. That, in turn, may set in motion a stressful day without recovery time at any point during it, thus creating less visible symptoms such as high blood pressure, headaches, or insomnia.

Exhaustion. The final stage in this process is exhaustion. The grind and its effects on your body, mind, and spirit leave you feeling—our current word of choice—wasted. This seems to be the paradigm for life as many people are living it today. One stressor follows another. Without recovery time, they mount and leave one physically tired, emotionally drained, and spiritually barren. An attorney friend recently described his own life in these very terms. He said, "The pace of my life doesn't leave me any time to recharge my batteries."

In *Through the Looking Glass*, Lewis Carroll has Alice say that "it takes all the running you can do to keep in the same place. If you want to get somewhere else, you must run at least twice as fast." Sounds familiar, doesn't it!

Research done in November of 1995 asked people across the United States to rank the top three priorities in their lives.[2] Here's what surfaced:

> 68% – Family life
>
> 46% – Spiritual life
>
> 44% – Health
>
> 25% – Financial situation
>
> 23% – Jobs
>
> 18% – Romantic life
>
> 14% – Leisure time
>
> 11% – Homes

Maybe the stress some of us feel relates directly to the fact that we tend to worry most over what matters least! To hear us tell it, family, faith, and health matter more than anything else. But watching us would make people think these things hardly matter at all when compared to work, mowing the grass, or skiing. By the way, how stressful is work? Take the following test, adapted from *Toxic Work* by Barbara Bailey Reinhold.

> Rate each of the following from 1 (almost never) to 4 (almost always):
>
> ___ I'm worried I won't find another job if I lose this one.
>
> ___ I wake up worrying about work.

___ I'm upset about the increased demands at work.

___ I find myself getting irritable or angry.

___ I speed impatiently from one task to another.

___ I don't have enough control over how I do my work.

___ I don't feel trusted and appreciated at work.

___ I'm worrying about whether I can keep up at work.

___ I wonder whether I'm really doing a good enough job.

___ It seems that nobody wants to know what I'm feeling.

___ I have trouble knowing what I'm really feeling.

___ I hold in my feelings until they finally erupt in some way.

___ It's hard to make enough time for friends and family.

___ People close to me complain that I'm not available enough.

___ I'm too worn out to give much time to my relationships.

If your score is under 25, you're probably managing stress well. If between 25–34, you could be in for emotional and physical discomfort; between 35–44, talk with others at work about ways to reduce stress. If the score is over 45, you are probably under a doctor's care but should consider a career counselor as well.[3]

Several high-profile people have chosen to reaffirm their priorities in order to cope with stress. Jeffrey Stiefler, president of American Express, quit his job to "work a less intense pace and spend more time with my family." William Galston walked away from his White House post as a presidential adviser when his ten-year-old son wrote him this letter: "Baseball's not fun when there's no one there to applaud you." Movie director Steven Spielberg observes the Sabbath faithfully and comes home from work at 6 P.M. daily to be with his wife and children.

HOW JESUS LIVED

Have you ever thought of Jesus' life in terms of the stress around him? True, he didn't have a cellular phone or e-mail. But he had a major dose of stress through the course of his life among us.

He was born in peril as a paranoid Herod the Great sought to have him killed.[4] Before you reply to offer that an infant isn't aware of the peril his parents feel, think again. Infants and small children are organic barometers to the emotional climate of their families. As Joseph and Mary fled to Egypt and had to live in a strange environment, the infant surely sensed it and suffered for it.

Then there was family stress for him as he grew up in Nazareth. Do you remember the comment in the Gospels that "his own brothers did not believe in him" prior to the resurrection?[5] What impact does it have on siblings today when one of them is taunted or mistreated within the group? Family is supposed to be a safe place, but it wasn't for Jesus—any more than it is for some people today.

Then begin to factor in the stresses of his public ministry. It began with forty days of fasting and temptation at the hands of Satan himself.[6] No man was ever subjected to such pressure, assaults, and slander. You can be sure of that because God does not allow anyone to be tempted beyond his ability to withstand it.[7] Since Jesus was the spiritually strongest person who has ever lived, Satan was allowed to pull out all the stops when confronting him.

As he moved among the masses of humanity for more than three years, there were the constant pressures of teaching, answering questions, and responding to challenges. Some attacked him as a demon-possessed man. Others were always setting traps for him. His critics and enemies questioned his motives. They called him insane and disloyal to the Law of Moses. And there eventually arose a group that was determined to kill him.

All these things taken collectively were in some sense surely worse than the final twenty-four hours of his stress-filled life. Without the ability to conquer the daily pressures that assaulted him, there would have been no single, defining moment such as Calvary.

Remember the point made earlier: It is not the crisis event so much as the grinding pressure of day-to-day stress that breaks people. Surely this was true of Jesus as well as the rest of us.

WHAT JESUS TAUGHT

Among the many things Jesus taught that relate to this issue, no single text is so critical as one in the Sermon on the Mount.

> Therefore I tell you, do not worry about your life, what you will eat or drink; or about your body, what you will wear. Is not life more important than food, and the body more important than clothes? Look at the birds of the air; they do not sow or reap or store away in barns, and yet your heavenly Father feeds them. Are you not much more valuable than they? Who of you by worrying can add a single hour to his life?
>
> And why do you worry about clothes? See how the lilies of the field grow. They do not labor or spin. Yet I tell you that not even Solomon in all his splendor was dressed like one of these. If that is how God clothes the grass of the field, which is here today and tomorrow is thrown into the fire, will he not much more clothe you, O you of little faith? So do not worry, saying "What shall we eat?" or "What shall we drink?" or "What shall we wear?" For the pagans run after all these things, and your heavenly Father knows that you need them. But seek first his kingdom and his righteousness, and all these things will be given to you as well. Therefore do not worry about tomorrow, for tomorrow will worry about itself. Each day has enough trouble of its own.[8]

In his book, *Matthew,* Myron Augsburger has summarized this material under three headings.

1. Worry is irreverent. Jesus declares that our tendency to welcome stress through worry is irreverent. That is, it fails to honor the fact that God is sovereign over all things. He gave us life, and he is sustaining it. He knows our needs, and he has promised to supply them within his will for our lives. Would that we were as wise as the birds who know that God is going to see that they get fed each day. Would that we trusted our heavenly Father enough to know that he will not abandon his people.

2. Worry is irrelevant. Second, Jesus says that worry is irrelevant. Half the things people worry about will never come to pass, and another 40 percent of life's troubles couldn't be averted by all the worry in the world. So it seems better to face today's real challenges than to worry about a tomorrow that may never come. That's why Jesus said that, "Each day has enough trouble of its own," and told us not to worry about tomorrow.

3. Worry is irresponsible. Finally, Jesus says that stress-producing worry is irresponsible. Anxiety will not empty tomorrow of its troubles, and it will rob today of its focus and energy. It distracts us from our present responsibilities and creates problems that otherwise could have been avoided. "Who of you by worrying can add a single hour to his life?" You can't add hours to your life by worry, but worry will take them off.[9]

There are some practical ways to reduce your stress in addition to stopping your worrying. Here are ten:

1. Plan some idleness every day.

2. Listen to others without interruption.

3. Read books that demand concentration.

4. Learn to savor food.

5. Have a place for retreat at home.

6. Avoid irritating, overly competitive people.

7. Plan leisurely, less-structured vacations.

8. Concentrate on enriching yourself.

9. Live by the calendar, not the stop watch.

10. Concentrate on one task at a time.[10]

Trying to summarize and pull together the insights Jesus gives us about coping with life's stressors, here are a half-dozen suggestions that seem appropriate.

1. Rely on God. Let life's challenges teach you to rely on God and his divine resources. By this point, I may have convinced you that your great need is to insulate yourself from stress. Sorry, I didn't make myself clear. For one thing, you can't get away from stress. For another, you need some in your life. Stress adds flavor and opportunity to human life. Stress isn't the problem. The problem is the fruitless worry over your stress and the failure to surrender it to God. The mistake we often make is trying to go it alone—fighting Satan and his host of spiritual evils with the resources of the flesh. "God is our refuge and strength, an ever-present help in trouble."[11] "That is why, for Christ's sake, I delight in weaknesses, in insults, in hardships, in persecutions, in difficulties," wrote Paul. "For when I am weak, then I am strong."[12] When life's accumulating stresses teach us the meaning of this verse, they have served us well. "Cast all your anxiety on him because he cares for you."[13]

2. Enjoy the little blessings of life. Learn to pay attention to the little payoffs life is giving you each day. Always looking ahead for the "big break" or the "big payoff" keeps many people from enjoying the satisfactions available to them right now. That seems to be at the heart of Paul's counsel: "But godliness with contentment is great gain. . . . But if we have food and clothing, we will be content with that."[14] You may already be familiar with the following piece—written by an anonymous friar in a Nebraska monastery late in his life—but it serves as a good reminder about how we sometimes miss the little things that give joy.

If I had my life to live over again, I'd try to make more mistakes next time.

I would relax, I would limber up, I would be sillier than I
have been this trip.

I know of very few things I would take seriously.

I would take more trips. I would be crazier.

I would climb more mountains, swim more rivers, and
watch more sunsets.

I would do more walking and looking.

I would eat more ice cream and less beans.

I would have more actual troubles, and fewer imaginary
ones.

You see, I'm one of those people who lives life prophylac-
tically and sensibly hour after hour, day after day.
Oh, I've had my moments, and if I had to do it over
again, I'd have more of them.

In fact, I'd try to have nothing else, just moments, one
after another, instead of living so many years ahead
each day. I've been one of those people who never
goes anywhere without a thermometer, a hot-water
bottle, a gargle, a raincoat, aspirin, and a parachute.

If I had to do it over again, I would go places, do things,
and travel lighter than I have.

If I had my life to live over, I would start barefooted earlier in the spring and stay that way later in the fall.

I would play hooky more.

I wouldn't make such good grades, except by accident.

I would ride on more merry-go-rounds.

I'd pick more daisies.

3. *Build a close network of family and friends.* Life is not about
things. It's about people and the relationships we can build with
them. Going back to the tragic case of Admiral Michael Boorda,
the newspaper editorial quoted earlier included this sentence:
"The tragedy is, as is often the case with suicide, Boorda apparently didn't let others in on his pain and didn't ask for their help."
We human beings really do need each other! "Carry each other's

burdens, and in this way you will fulfill the law of Christ." The "law of Christ" seems to be essentially about loving one another as an extension of our love for God,[15] and we cannot fulfill it by trying to live as a world of Lone Rangers.

4. *Cultivate a sense of humor.* The late Erma Bombeck wrote bestsellers with titles like *The Grass Is Always Greener over the Septic Tank* and *When You Look Like Your Passport Photo, It's Time to Go Home.* Her father died when she was only nine years old. At twenty she was found to have a hereditary kidney disorder that would eventually lead to kidney failure. (Two of her three children have inherited the problem.) In 1991 she had breast cancer and underwent a mastectomy. In 1993 she started four-times-a-day peritoneal dialysis until she received a kidney transplant almost three years later. Complications from the transplant took her life. I suspect her sense of humor was a coping device. It helped her deal with her pain. It kept her from getting brittle and grumpy. It helped her live sixty-nine years in a positive rather than negative way, with joy rather than self-pity.

People who succeed with life tend to have a great sense of humor. It gets them through the tough times. Remember what Ronald Reagan said when he was shot in 1981? "Honey, I forgot to duck," he told Nancy at the hospital. To the surgeons about to operate on him, he said, "Please tell me you're Republicans." A sense of humor is great therapy when you hit a bump in the road—and everybody's road has some bumps. "A cheerful heart is good medicine, but a crushed spirit dries up the bones."[16]

5. *Learn to be flexible.* Stress relates to change. Altered circumstances require us to change and thereby put us under stress. Dr. Hans Selye, a recognized expert in the field, defines physical reactions to stress as "nonspecific response of the body to a demand." Learning to be flexible is a must. The people who suffer the most negative effects from stress are the set-in-concrete personalities who fight change. But change can be growth. So when your plans change for whatever reasons, look for a way to use your new situation constructively.[17] Fretting that you aren't in control is a sure

source of anxiety. As the old farmer advised the city fellow, "Don't take life so seriously, son. You'll never get out of it alive."

6. *Take charge of your life by the power and grace of God.* When you feel the drawn-tight effects of stress in your life, deal with it. Don't fret and foam at the mouth. Do something! Stop smoking. Begin exercising and losing some weight. Read a book, learn how to use a computer, or start saving money to skydive. Repair an old friendship, or seek out a new one. Get out of the criticizing business with your mate, company, or church; be part of making the situation better. "For God did not give us a spirit of timidity, but a spirit of power, of love and of self-discipline."[18]

You'll never get away from stress on planet earth. Jesus confirmed, "In this world you will have trouble." He continued by saying: "But take heart! I have overcome the world."[19]

What this world dishes out doesn't have to destroy us. With the mind of Christ to inform ours, we can share in his victory over whatever the world throws at us.

The problem is, they keep coming up with technology nobody asks for. They believe we want Freeze-Frame Search, and Split Screen, and 14-Day Timers. Clocks that make coffee and cameras that talk. We don't want that. You know what I want? I just want to lie down. That's really all I want. If I could lie down for a half-hour. That's really all I want. If I could lie down for a half-hour, I'd be so happy. I've been reading instructions since 1987; my head is pounding. I can't do it. . . . I want to write a letter.

"Dear Japan, STOP!!! We're fine. This is plenty of stuff. Why don't you stop with the VCRs and work on diseases. Go cure a disease—I'm going to figure out my cordless phone."

Paul Riser, *Couplehood*

Money

Richard Leider learned more about what he didn't need while backpacking in East Africa than about what he did need. His state-of-the-art pack was crammed full with every modern gadget money could buy. What a contrast to the "loa" of his group's guide, a Masai chief—one knife and one stick.

At the end of the day, Leider noticed that he was exhausted while the chief was ready for more. When the Masai guide asked to see all the gadgets, Leider complied and then explained why each item was crucial.

"But does it make you happy?" the chief kept wanting to know. Leider wound up ditching half of the stuff in one of the villages.[1]

Have you ever had the feeling that you're packing too much? Could you lighten the load a bit and feel fresher?

That's hard to do in our culture, because we live with two very powerful myths:

- *Myth #1: Now is better.* Grab it at the drive-through window. Nuke it in the microwave. Buy it now and don't make your first payment for six months. The principle of delayed gratification means no more to most of us adults than it does to a three-year-old on Halloween night with a sack full of candy.

- *Myth #2: More is better.* The more you make, the more you buy, the bigger your house, the more exotic your vacation. More will somehow make your life better.

But the "more is better" philosophy leaves people with endless frustration. Why? Because they never get enough. They continue redefining "more" and keep pushing. In the meantime, they miss the joy that surrounds them. Laurence Shames was right on target when he made this observation about our hunger for more:

> Consumption kept the workers working, which kept the paychecks coming, which kept the people spending, which kept inventors inventing and investors investing, which meant there was more to consume. . . . It was a perfect circle, complete in itself—but empty in the middle.[2]

The Western lust for more by both the "haves" and the "have-not-yets" is clearly out of control. It is built on the terrible illusion that more things bring more life. We have confused life with lifestyle.

Christ followers are called in a different direction. Jesus gave many specific warnings about the power of money to control us.

His words and his life come to us not as clouds raining on our party of accumulation and affluence but as a bright light showing us a way out of the chaos and insanity that surround us.

WHAT JESUS TAUGHT

A person reading the Gospels is quickly struck by the seemingly "antimoney" sayings of Jesus:

- Blessed are you who are poor, for yours is the kingdom of God. . . . But woe to you who are rich, for you have already received your comfort.
- Do not store up for yourselves treasures on earth.
- If you want to be perfect, go, sell your possessions and give to the poor, and you will have treasure in heaven. Then come, follow me.
- It is hard for a rich man to enter the kingdom of heaven.
- Watch out! Be on your guard against all kinds of greed; a man's life does not consist in the abundance of his possessions.[3]

It's evident that Jesus considers money a dangerous topic. But is he truly antimoney? No! A closer look at his teaching shows that he is seeking to shift our understanding of wealth from the short-sighted "now is better" and "more is better" perspectives of our culture to a perspective more in harmony with God's intentions.

TRUST GOD NOT MONEY

Throughout Jesus' teaching about money, there is one overriding concern: that we place our trust in God alone and not in wealth, power, or prestige.

Do not store up for yourselves treasures on earth, where moth and rust destroy, and where thieves break in and steal. But store up for yourselves treasures in heaven, where moth and rust do not destroy, and where thieves do not break in and steal. For where your treasure is, there your heart will be also. . . . No one can serve two masters. Either he will hate the one and love the other, or he will be devoted to the one and despise the other. You cannot serve both God and Money.[4]

As Christians, we must face the issue of selfish accumulation of goods in a world of limited resources. And we must meet head-on the question of selfish, extravagant lifestyles when the needs of kingdom building are so great.

Jesus consistently focuses on an even more important question: *Where are we placing our trust?* "A [person's] life does not consist in the abundance of . . . possessions," he exclaimed.[5] Nothing money can buy can offer ultimate life or happiness.

With good reason, Scripture warns again and again about idolatry. Idolatry is our greatest temptation. We are tempted to try to find life in someone or something other than God. Some attempt to do so with a god made of wood. Others try to squeeze life out of another person (and then another, then another), and others try to find it in money and "better" lifestyles.

Those who try to find life through a bigger house, a nicer car, a fatter retirement fund, newer furniture, or a longer vacation are destined to be disappointed. While any of these could provide enjoyment for someone who already has found "abundant life," none are capable of filling the empty hole for those who haven't.

One more trip to the mall cannot fix you. Money can buy:

- sex, but not intimacy
- a house, but not peace
- medicine, but not health
- amusement, but not joy
- therapy, but not healing
- a bed, but not sleep
- allies, but not friends

When Jesus met people who were putting their trust in their wealth, his solution was radical surgery. "Sell everything you've got, give away your money, and then come follow me," he told one young man. He knew that we cannot serve two masters—both God and Money. The first commandment, "You shall have no other gods beside me," demands that our full allegiance go to God. He alone can give us life.

Of course, this seems to give everyone an easy out. "I'm not trying to find life in my possessions. I'm just enjoying them," most will object. Maybe we need to ask some critical questions:

- What do you think about more often when your mind is in neutral: how to follow God or how to obtain something you've been wanting?

- How many hours a week are you devoting to advancing your career and how much time in quiet communion with God?

- What feelings do you have when you sense God's conviction to give away a large percentage of what you have?

- If everything you had were taken away, what would this do to your sense of joy and completeness?

- How much of your self-esteem is dependent upon your career, income, and possessions?

Remember, the American Dream is not the Christ follower's dream! One Christian university student was recently asked what his dream was. The published response was, "To be able to buy whatever I want, whenever I want it, without having to worry about running out of money." And Christ died for that dream? No way.

Of course, we shouldn't blame this one student alone. Somehow he managed to live in a Christian home, attend a Christian church, and get a Christian education without having that dream challenged.

Jesus thankfully took us beneath all the surface issues to find what's ultimately at stake—where we place our trust. "But seek first his kingdom and his righteousness, and all these things will be given to you as well," he promised.[6]

As we try to live as Jesus would live today, an important question is, "What will the test of time do to the object of our trust and affection?" If our deepest treasures can be destroyed by nature (moth), time (rust), or humans (theft), they aren't eternal treasures. "What good will it be for a man if he gains the whole world, yet forfeits his soul?" he asked.[7]

I recently saw a cartoon that pictured a woman bringing flowers to the cemetery. She came to her husband's tombstone which read:

R. J. HARWELL

Born 1914

Gave up smoking 1959

Gave up booze 1973

Gave up red meat 1983

Gave up fried foods 1990

Started walking regularly 1992

Died anyway 1995

Nothing we do can exempt us from eternity's testing. That's maybe the most valuable lesson of Monopoly. At the end of the game, the board is folded, everything is put away, and the lid is placed on top. It's a little reminder that someday our lives will be over as well. Then it will hardly matter who owned how many railroads and utilities, or even Boardwalk.

WE ARE STEWARDS NOT OWNERS

A second critical concern of Jesus' is that we remember that our wealth is really God's wealth. We are stewards rather than owners. He considers riches to be neither evil nor good, but creations from God that have been entrusted to us for his use.

The story Jesus tells at the beginning of Luke 16 has a rather strange hero: a manager who in many ways was a scoundrel. He had wasted his master's possessions, not just by incompetence or negligence but by dishonesty.[8]

When the rich landowner told him to clear out his desk and get out (impromptu downsizing!), the man put up no self-defense. Instead, he had a little talk with himself. He had three choices: (1) He could beg, but that was beneath him. (2) He could do manual labor, but he already had back problems. (3) Before word of his dismissal could spread, he could make friends who would help him in the future.

He began calling in people who owed the wealthy landowner.

"How much do you owe? Eight hundred gallons of olive oil? Well, this is your lucky day! Cut your bill in half."

"And what do you owe? A thousand bushels of wheat? Well, this is 20 Percent Tuesday. Give yourself a 20 percent discount."

No doubt word spread rapidly about what a magnanimous person the wealthy owner was—not a big rip-off, aristocratic swine like so many others. No sir, he really cared about his debtors.

This left the rich guy with an interesting choice: (1) He could tell everyone it was a mistake, thereby upsetting them and ruining his reputation. (2) He could swallow the losses and enjoy the praise.

Having chosen the latter, he called in his former manager and said: "For a lying dog, that was pretty good" (loose translation).

This strange parable can be understood only by looking at its perspective on money and stewardship:

> Whoever can be trusted with very little can also be trusted with much, and whoever is dishonest with very little will also be dishonest with much. So if you have not been trustworthy in handling worldly wealth, who will

trust you with true riches? And if you have not been trustworthy with someone else's property, who will give you
property of your own?[9]

What we have isn't really ours. Your bank account isn't ultimately yours; nor is your car. "The earth is the Lord's, and everything in it" is the perspective of Jesus, as well as of the psalmist.[10]

God is the owner of everything. If he wants to play King of the
Mountain, he can use his backyard: the Rockies, the Andes, the
Alps, or the Himalayas. If he wants to take a dip in the pool, he can
pick from the Pacific or the Atlantic, the Indian or the Arctic. If he
needs a bit of running water, he can choose from the Nile, the Mississippi, the Amazon, or the Colorado. All are his!

I've read the literature that warns against trying to make this
appeal to baby boomers because it doesn't motivate them to give.
But that doesn't matter. It's true! The pronoun "your" must be
used carefully when speaking of your money, your car, your
clothes, your house, your investments, or your time.

The landowner's money manager is praised for his prudence:
He used present opportunities to insure future welfare. Every steward must do that—though usually in more conventional ways.

In the following story, Jesus underscores the eternal conse-
quence of failing to use God's money for his purposes. He tells of
a wealthy man who refused to care for the beggar Lazarus. His
soul-condemning sin wasn't wealth, but a greedy and uncompas-
sionate heart. He was able to look at someone starving without
feeling a sword pierce his heart. He failed to manage God's wealth
in a way that helped one who was suffering in his presence. The
rich man didn't run Lazarus off; he just quietly ignored him.[11]

Behind all of Jesus' instruction concerning money, then, are
these two concerns:

1. that we place our trust in God, looking to him alone for
life

2. that we remember God's trust in us, having made us
stewards of his possessions

HOW JESUS LIVED

Even if we didn't have Jesus' pointed instructions about money, we could have learned these two principles by looking carefully at his life. His simple life was in complete harmony with his teaching. He refused to get caught up in the "more is better" game. He never tried to squeeze life out of things.

"Foxes have holes and birds of the air have nests, but the Son of Man has no place to lay his head," he told a would-be follower.[12] He trusted his heavenly Father to provide for his daily bread and thankfully received some support from a few women who had been healed through his power.[13]

Many world leaders have been buried with vast fortunes and wealth that testified to their power and glory. But when the King of Glory was crucified, he left only a few garments for the soldiers to claim.

And yet, no one has ever been more full of life! He not only warned his followers that life wasn't found in the abundance of possessions but also told them where true life was.

When Jesus drew up his will for his disciples, he left them fabulously rich with gifts like:

- the Holy Spirit[14]
- peace[15]
- devoted love[16]
- eternal life[17]
- the promise of eternal glory[18]

He prayed for them, "Father, I want those you have given me to be with me where I am, and to see my glory, the glory you have given me because you loved me before the creation of the world."[19] Such a prayer testifies to the life of one who lived life to the fullest degree.

The whole story of Jesus' life is amazing when you back away from it far enough to see how much he gave up because of his incredible love. One of his followers, Paul, reflected on his selfless love: "For you know the grace of our Lord Jesus Christ, that though he was rich, yet for your sakes he became poor, so that you through his poverty might become rich."[20]

Jesus was the incarnate illustration of what a life that seeks God and his righteousness rather than this world's treasures looks like.

WHERE HE LEADS I WILL FOLLOW

Where, then, will following Jesus lead us in our relationship with money?

1. THE PATH OF SIMPLICITY

Those who walk in the steps of one who had no place to lay his head must surely see the value of a simple, unencumbered life.

But two precautions are in order. First, simplicity and poverty aren't necessarily the same. I, for one, have invested too much time in hyper-introspection and guilt over the level of my lifestyle. God intends for us to pray seriously about this but not to live in guilt and defeat over it. "Condemnation and guilt over mere possession has no part in scriptural faith and is, in the end, only a barrier to the right use of the riches of the earth," Dallas Willard warns.[21]

Second, be aware that your decision of what lifestyle is appropriate for you must not be made binding on others. They, too, must prayerfully decide for themselves.

2. THE PATH OF CONTENTMENT

A bigger concern than how many square feet our house should have or how expensive our car should be (since someone can always outhumble you anyway!) is our willingness to be content. Would your life still be rich and full if suddenly much was taken from you? Do you live with Paul's take-it-or-leave-it attitude?

I have learned to be content whatever the circumstances. I know what it is to be in need, and I know what it is to have plenty. I have learned the secret of being content in any and every situation, whether well fed or hungry, whether living in plenty or in want. I can do everything through him who gives me strength.[22]

3. THE PATH OF GENEROSITY

We know many wonderful stories of Christian men and women who give generously (out of their wealth or their poverty!) to fund mission work, inner-city ministries, and Christian publications. We know of many who give to their local church a tithe (and more) of their income.

I'll never forget the day a young man heard in chapel at his university about a mentally handicapped woman who loved music. The person introducing her mentioned that she wasn't able to enjoy her music at the time because someone had stolen her tape player. As soon as chapel was over, the student rushed back to his dorm, grabbed his new stereo (which had been a graduation present), took it back to the chapel, and quietly left it for the woman. "It is more blessed to give than to receive."

4. THE PATH OF TRUST

This is the ultimate path. In traveling this path, we'll remember that only God through his Son, Jesus Christ, can give us life.

GAINING WHAT CAN'T BE LOST

In 1956 Auca Indians in Ecuador killed five missionaries who were trying to tell them the good news about Jesus. Nine kids lost their fathers that day. But their lives were not in vain. One of them, Jim Elliot, had lived with a motto that fits this chapter well: "He is no fool who gives what he cannot keep to gain what he cannot lose."

What are you seeking to give away for the cause of the kingdom? And what are you trying desperately to gain? "For to me, to live is Christ," Paul explained. Then, because his life centered on Jesus Christ, he added, "and to die is gain."[23]

That's a hope that money can't buy!

My parents were content with me if I tried to do as well as I could what I was able to do. I wasn't compared with others whether they were more gifted than I or less gifted. . . . That seems like sound common sense, sound psychology and sound Christianity.

Andrew M. Greely, *Confessions of a Parish Priest*

Competition

Much that is good about the United States is built on competition. So is much of what is bad. Let me explain. Competition in free markets tends to improve the quality of products. When Eastman Kodak entered the copier market several years ago, it forced Xerox to improve its quality. Fuzzy images got sharper when a well-financed competitor forced the people who had held a near monopoly on the copier market to compete on quality rather than price cutting.

Competition in the marketplace also serves to protect consumers. Business cannot gouge the public when aggressive competitors are trying to beat them at their own game. Who among us hasn't benefited from both short-term price wars among gasoline stations and the more significant contest for a market share among automobile, home appliance, or computer manufacturers?

We celebrate and epitomize the competitive spirit in athletics. In the storied history of the Olympic Games, there have been many memorable moments when courage and persistence inspired all of us. My home state of Tennessee still celebrates the late Wilma Rudolph, the first American woman to win three gold medals in one Olympic Games back in 1960. Rudolph was the twentieth of twenty-two children, had both scarlet fever and polio as a little girl, and rose above doctors' predictions that she might never walk again to become a track superstar.

In the Atlanta Games in the summer of 1996, gymnast Kerri Strug emerged as America's darling. With two Russian performances yet to be attempted and the gold medal still in doubt, she guaranteed a first-place finish for the U.S. women gymnasts. On her first vault, the four-foot-nine-inch athlete heard her ankle snap and had to limp off the floor. Perhaps she should have removed herself from the competition to avoid further injury, but she didn't. She pulled herself together, set herself for a final attempt, and nailed a near-perfect vault before a cheering crowd. Told she was a hero for what she had done, Kerri Strug was reluctant. "Everybody keeps telling me I am," she said. "I just felt like I had to do it. I owed it to everyone."

Competition can create better products. It can make things more affordable. And it can inspire the human spirit to soar. But it also has a downside. Competition can generate backstabbing practices, litigation, and more pages of government regulations that in turn create waste and inefficiency.

It is the dark side of competition that generates corporate spying and outrageous lies. Remember the rumors of a few years ago about worms in a fast-food chain's burgers? And what about the rumor about Proctor & Gamble's logo being associated with Satan worship?

Athletic competition was once promoted for the sake of virtues such as honesty, fair play, and teamwork. Today it is hard to keep a straight face when using those words in relation to such characters as Mike Tyson, Tanya Harding, Dennis Rodman, or Roberto Alomar. The old maxim about athletics was straightforward and simple. Although it still makes good ethical sense, it isn't heard very often anymore. I wonder if today's schoolchildren could recite it: "It isn't whether you win or lose, but how you play the game that counts." Today's win-at-any-cost philosophy long ago trickled down to college athletics, Little League, and schoolyard competition. Embarrassing stories of cheating, fighting, and various other ways sports are corrupt make the news regularly.

When an Oakland Raider's fan bit off part of the ear of a San Diego Chargers fan, Municipal Court Judge Ann Winebrenner sentenced the thirty-year-old fan to 180 days in prison. "Screaming and yelling in a bar about what football team is going to beat another football team is, in my mind, absolutely inane as a source of provocation."[1]

What is the mind of Christ in all this? Are all forms of competition wrong and to be avoided by Christians? Are there any practical guidelines that can help us negotiate these troubled waters?

How Jesus Lived

Believe it or not, Jesus had to deal with this problem in a variety of forms. If we watch and listen to him, several helpful insights will emerge. Here are some forms of competition that Jesus faced in his life.

FAMILY COMPETITION

Jesus unquestionably faced competitive strife in his own family. After he had begun his public ministry of teaching and working miracles of compassion, his brothers mocked and taunted him about his claims. As the fall Festival of Tabernacles approached, James, Joseph, Simon, and Jude hit him with this: "You ought to leave here and go to Judea, so that your disciples may see the miracles you do. No one who wants to become a public figure acts in secret. Since you are doing these things, show yourself to the world."[2]

Lest anyone read these lines about his brothers' comments as supportive, John explains that "his own brothers did not believe in him."[3] So their challenge for Jesus to present himself to the huge crowds assembling in Jerusalem for the most popular of the Jewish feasts was a put-down, a sarcastic challenge.

Have you ever thought what it must have been like to live in that sort of family? Jesus' brothers were in-house skeptics at best. On their worst days, they competed with him both as to his understanding of Scripture and his own self-understanding.

What an argument against Jesus it must have been for his critics to point out that even his own brothers were not sympathetic to him.

Their "advice" to Jesus in this setting was fleshly, carnal advice to a spiritual man. In effect, they dared him to enter the Holy City and compete with the other teachers and alleged miracle workers. Thinking in the only terms they really understood at the time, Jesus' siblings thought he should make good on his claims (which they rejected!) by outdoing the other preachers.

ECONOMIC COMPETITION

Jesus was also forced to deal with the ugly competitiveness that greed always generates. For example, once while he was preaching, he was interrupted by a man whose mind was on anything but the Lord's sermon. "Teacher, tell my brother to divide the inheritance with me," came the intrusion.[4]

Rabbis were frequently consulted to settle ethical disputes. So here was a man who heard of the new rabbi, thought of his old complaint, and sought him out for the sake of dragging him into the controversy. Was his complaint legitimate? Had his brother cheated him? We'll never know, for Jesus chose not to address the facts of the case but the man's underlying motivation—greed.

The Parable of the Rich Fool that Jesus gave in this setting was designed to call attention to the ultimate correction for rivalry, unholy competition, and greed—being "rich toward God." Everyone needs to bear in mind that his or her relationship with God matters more than the medals, fame, or money we compete with one another to gain. None of these things will have any ultimate value for someone who does not know Christ as Savior.

RELIGIOUS COMPETITION

Then Jesus encountered a form of competition that sprang from the religious insecurities of his own disciples. They came to the Master one day and told about their encounter with another believer who was doing things in the name of Jesus. John acted as their spokesman and said, "Teacher, we saw a man driving out demons in your name and we told him to stop, because he was not one of us."[5] They rebuked the man because they saw him as their competitor.

One should note in passing that the man was not rebuked for making false claims about his ability to cast out demons. Neither was he challenged because of anything heretical he was teaching about Jesus. The disciples told him to stop his ministry for no reason other than his nonalignment with their little group.

What makes people do this sort of thing? Surely the answer is insecurity. If the little group that had been traveling with Jesus really knew him and felt secure in their relationship with him, they would have had no motivation to hinder someone else's ministry. Only someone who fears he has no light in himself feels compelled to blow out some other person's candle.

WHAT JESUS TAUGHT

The response of Jesus to these situations of family, economic, and religious competition was consistent. He did nothing to encourage or fuel the strife. Beyond that, he showed how unnecessary and wrong these forms of conflict are.

To summarize Jesus' teachings about competition, he basically taught his followers to seek peace, avoid selfishness, and never inflict unnecessary harm. As to the specific situations listed above, notice how he responded to each of them.

FAMILY COMPETITION

Jesus had a competitive, dysfunctional family life. How did he handle it? For one thing, he knew that nothing short of the resurrection was going to change his brothers' minds about him. So he accepted that, focused on the work the Father had given him to do, and found a new "extended family" for himself. He refused to neglect his ministry or waste his time trying to change what couldn't be changed.

One day Jesus was teaching large crowds of people, and his mother and brothers came to see him. Because of the number of people crowded around him, they could not make their way through to get his attention. When someone told him that his family wanted to speak with him, this was his reply: "My mother and brothers are those who hear God's word and put it into practice."[6]

It would be a mistake to read this response as an insensitive, uncaring one. Jesus was certainly never disrespectful toward his mother—regardless of his brothers' feelings toward him. His behavior does not mean that family is unimportant or can be ignored, but it does mean that the relationships that grow out of spiritual life and duty take precedence over all others. One must not allow family issues of tension, misunderstanding, or dysfunction to stand in the way of carrying through with the duty of honoring our heavenly Father in all things. His words on this point are both clear and compelling.

ECONOMIC COMPETITION

Jesus' teaching about selfishness—especially as it relates to money and possessions—makes it clear that it is sometimes better to be wronged and cheated than to become obsessed with "getting my fair share."[7] I have watched people destroy their spiritual lives in order to fight a business partner in court or to get what they believed they were entitled to have from an employer. While I have no skill to judge the legal merits of such cases, I have learned over time what Jesus saw immediately in the man who interrupted his sermon that day: The motivation behind all such wranglings is (or quickly becomes) greed rather than justice.

In the Parable of the Rich Fool, Jesus asks us to envision a farmer who had prospered greatly planning his future. The story has the man worrying about "my crops," "my barns," "my grain," "my goods," and "myself." The one thing he didn't consider was God's sovereignty and ownership of everything. So, when he died that night, everything that had been important to him was lost— including his soul. "This is how it will be with anyone who stores up things for himself but is not rich toward God," said Jesus.[8] It isn't having that is sinful, but hoarding.

This story has its modern counterpart in *The Forbes Four Hundred List* of wealthiest Americans. When Ted Turner gave $200 million to charity in 1994, he admits, "My hand shook when I signed the papers because I knew I was taking myself out of the running for the richest man in America." (Wonder what his hand did when he signed over $1 billion to United Nations charities in September of 1997?) His theory is that the *Forbes* list "is destroying our country" by encouraging hoarding rather than sharing. He suggests an annual list of most generous Americans to replace it, offering an "Ebenezer Scrooge Prize" to embarrass stingy billionaires and "Heart of Gold Awards" to honor philanthropists.[9]

The part confession and part challenge from Ted Turner illustrates that much of the greed that infects our culture is directly linked to competitiveness. One person wants to be richer than another, wants to be higher on the list of "haves" than his neighbor, or wants to be a greater "success" than anyone else in his field.

RELIGIOUS COMPETITION

What Jesus said about religious insecurity and the competition it generates must have caught his disciples off guard. It seems clear that John and his fellow disciples thought they had done a good thing by trying to silence and shut down their "competition." They appear to have been expecting Jesus to compliment what they had done. Instead, this is what he said: "Do not stop him. No one who does a miracle in my name can in the next moment say anything bad about me, for whoever is not against us is for us."[10]

The world is full of people with the spirit of these disciples. In order to feel good about their own relationship with the Lord, they somehow feel it is necessary to question or reject someone else's. What is there about our sinful nature that drives us to such behavior, if not ugly competitiveness?

WHAT JESUS OFFERS

Set over against all these negatives, Jesus offers us an alternative way to go at life. It is a way that eliminates unholy competition.

RESTRAINT IN RELATIONSHIPS

Cute, blond, five-year-old Lindsey went to kindergarten. Her parents received a phone call from her teacher in February. If you have children, you know the somersaults your stomach can do when a teacher calls!

"We made valentines at school today, and most of the children made them for Mom or Dad or someone who was obviously very special to them," the teacher said. "When I walked by where Lindsey was working, she had written 'Anthony' across the top of hers."

The teacher explained that Anthony was a little boy in her class who had picked on Lindsey and made her life unpleasant. He had been told that what he was doing was wrong and not to do it again. He had even been punished for his misbehavior. But he had persisted. So a startled teacher asked, "Lindsey, why are you making your valentine for Anthony?"

"Well, Anthony has been mean to me," came a sweet-voiced reply. "So I thought that if I made him a special card, he'd be nice!"

What a wonderful alternative to the way some of us treat people who have mistreated us. We think in terms of getting even. At the very least, we don't put those people at the top of our list for special favors. But Lindsey did, and that is why Jesus told us to become like little children in order to enter the kingdom of God.[11]

Are you having a hard time with someone in your life? A client? A child? An employee? Have you already tried instruction, warning, and punishment? Perhaps it is time to do something radical by imitating Lindsey—and God.

CIVILITY IN THE COMMONPLACE

Seven hundred and forty kids participated in a youth basketball league in Texas in 1995. One Saturday, a little girl fouled out of the game with about three minutes left to play. Her grandmother, convinced that several of the fouls called against her were undeserved, was vocal in complaining. The girl's team wound up losing.

According to the custom of the league, at the end of the games the coaches had all the players line up to shake hands with the opposing team. The little girl who had fouled out, along with several of her teammates, spit into their hands as the handshaking started. Several mothers from the opposing team saw what was happening and began to talk about the poor sportsmanship on display.

The very verbal grandmother heard the comments, came over to one of the mothers, and told her that her daughter's team deserved to be spit on. The mother then told her to be quiet and called her an unflattering name. At that, the grandmother hit the mother in the jaw and knocked her backward. Both women had to be restrained, and the police were called.

And we wonder where the children pick up their attitudes and behaviors?

MORALITY IN THE MARKETPLACE

Yes, competitiveness is part of the business world. Some of the values of healthy competition were listed at the start of this chapter. It's the unhealthy competition that must be reined in, the mistreatment of people that must go.

The Iron Rule says that we must always win, be noticed, get our way, be special, and get a reward. This means, of course, that someone else has to lose, be overlooked, feel slighted, be treated as less important, and get squashed. Iron Rule people feel good about themselves only when they're on top of the heap and don't mind having to hurt others to stay there. Sounds terrible, doesn't it? Yet that is how some employers and managers treat their work force.

The Marshmallow Rule, by contrast, tells us to see ourselves as losers, never voice an opinion, always give in, regard ourselves as unworthy, and just make the best of things. Some have been taught this rule in the name of Christian "humility." These people are natural matches to Iron Rule folk—with Iron types eventually being repulsed by Marshmallow apathy, and Marshmallow types seething with anger at Iron arrogance. Marshmallows are eager to please and will do anything to keep the peace. They are taken advantage of at work and dumped on. They are compliant but angry, conforming but resentful.

By contrast, Christianity proposes a world of mutual respect where people look for ways to show respect for and bring benefit to all. It says that everyone's opinions and feelings matter. It teaches us that shared values, shared triumphs, and shared benefits are best. Win-win is a better strategy than win-lose.

Yet most of us continue to act as if we are obligated to compete and seem to feel that we are compelled to outdo someone else. What a waste of good energy. How unlike Christ's example and his Golden Rule: "Do to others what you would have them do to you."[12]

DETENTE AMONG BELIEVERS

It will be incredibly difficult for the Christians who read a book like this to model community, harmony, and civility in the other spheres of life if we cannot learn these lovely traits among ourselves. Our churches are too fragmented. Division reigns. Yet all of us know that division among Christians is not the will of God.

Perhaps we are confused because we have sought unity through institutional oneness, but there is no evidence that Jesus ever thought of creating an institution. The New Testament notion of the church is that of a living organism, a spiritual body with Christ as head. Or perhaps we should think of the church as a family. But it is definitely not an "institution," as we define the term. Living organisms and families can be whole and united with great variety, whereas institutions spawn clones of themselves.

Maybe part of our problem is that we still labor under a false illusion that the early church was something it never was. A doctrinally flawless and behaviorally pure church which was everywhere uniform no more existed in the days of first-century Jerusalem, Corinth, and Colossae than it does today. Yet they were a single brotherhood of believers, whereas we are not.

Again, it is possible that we have a romanticized notion of unity, which holds that a Christian cannot be one with people with whom he has doctrinal disagreements, whose commitments he cannot embrace, or whose projects he cannot share. Do you have parents or siblings, mate or children? Do you deny that these same differences exist among you? Yet you are still family, *one* family.

Others of us have a sneaking hunch that human pride is the fundamental root of our failure at unity. We are competitive in an ungodly way. Each of us has enough pride to insist that he or she is always right. I cannot see my own faults any easier than you can see yours. Thus, we hold each other at arm's length. We are civil with each other, but we will not embrace one another as brothers and sisters in Christ and affirm that we are one. Accepted by grace and cleansed by blood, people who make an orthodox confession of faith in Jesus must end the intramural bloodbaths that mock God's will for the unity of his people.

We must stop measuring faithfulness by the number of believers we have rejected or by the issues we have added to the gospel. While tempted to give way to strife, to compete with our brothers who do not cross their t's just so, we must remember that Jesus Christ is Lord of all.

Biblical scholar William Barclay desribes what happens to a church when Christ is dethroned.

> Eris [strife] invades the church and becomes charac-
> teristic of the church, when the leaders and the members
> of the church think more about people and about parties
> and about slogans and about personal issues than they do
> about Jesus Christ. Here is our warning. Whenever in a
> church Jesus Christ is dethroned from the central place,
> all personal relationships go wrong. When a man begins
> to preach, not to exalt Jesus Christ, but to exalt his own
> personal and private view of Jesus Christ, that is to say,
> when a man preaches a theology rather than a gospel,
> when a man begins to argue and demolish his opponent
> rather than to win him, then eris comes in.
>
> No sin more commonly invades the Church than eris;
> none is more destructive of Christian fellowship; but eris
> cannot even gain an entry to the Church, if Christ be
> supreme there.[13]

Out of Greek and Roman mythology, there is an ancient legend that tells how Hercules encountered a strange animal on a narrow road. He struck it with his club and passed on. Soon, however, the animal overtook him. Now three times as large at it was before, Hercules was seriously threatened by the animal and began to fight it with all his might. Each time he struck it, the animal grew even larger and deadlier.

Then Pallas appeared to Hercules and warned him to stop striking the animal. "The monster's name is Strife," she said. "Let it alone and it will soon become as little as it was at first."

Though only an ancient fable, this is important advice for anyone who thinks that by striking blows he can put an end to blows!

Set aside competitive strife and work toward love and unity with other believers.

The majority of us find it hard to get through a week without lying. One in five can't make it through a single day—and we're talking about conscious, premeditated lies. In fact, the way some people talk about trying to do without lies, you'd think that they were smokers trying to get through a day without a cigarette.

—James Patterson & Peter Kim, *The Day America Told the Truth*

CHAPTER SIX

Honesty

In the 1970s, a little-known governor from the South with a soft drawl made a Cinderella bid for the White House based not on his experience to run the country (he had little) but on a single, sincere promise: "I will never lie to you." For few other reasons, in the aftermath of Watergate, Americans embraced Jimmy Carter. A person who promises to tell the truth and who delivers on the promise is a person worth following!

It isn't hard for us to appreciate Diogenes' search through ancient Athens, as he sought an honest man. Lying is all around us. There is the head basketball coach who promises he won't leave and then three days later signs another contract for more money. Or the man who promises he'll be faithful "until death do us part" and then leaves for another woman. Then there is the politician who makes great promises about decreasing taxes while balancing the budget and then breaks her promises. No wonder one person with integrity sticks out.

Lee Strobel tells about a seven-year-old ballplayer from Florida named Tanner. In an important game (and aren't all Little League games vitally important?), Tanner was playing first base. When a grounder came at him, he reached out to tag the runner between first and second.

"You're out!" screamed the umpire.

Tanner looked at the ball, then to the ump. "Excuse me, sir. But I missed him."

"You didn't tag him?" the puzzled official asked. "Okay, then he's safe!"

You can imagine how this endeared the little guy to his teammates and coaches!

But a couple of weeks later Tanner was playing shortstop when another grounder came to him. After he stretched to tag the runner between second and third, the umpire—same one as before—yelled, "He's safe!"

The diminutive infielder looked at the ball for quite a while, then dejectedly tossed it back to the pitcher.

"Is something wrong?" the ump asked him.

"Yeah, I tagged him this time."

"Really? Okay, then *he's out!*"

The other team's manager came storming out of the dugout to protest, only to get this response: "Look, I know this little boy. Tanner tells the truth. If Tanner says he tagged your player, then he tagged him." Discussion over.

Can you imagine how unique a Tanner would be in our Pinocchio culture? What if he, as a young lawyer or accountant, started pointing out that his firm seemed to be billing clients for more hours than was right? Or what if he became an assistant editor for the *National Enquirer?* Can you picture him walking into the senior editor's office to object, "You know, I don't think we can prove that Elvis had a sex change and now works in the Senate." Or what if he were a university publicist, trying to bring truth and balance to alumni- and student-driven publications rather than half-truths and hype?

Contrast the story of Tanner with a more recognizable one—one recalled by Stephen Carter:

> A couple of years ago as I sat watching a football game with my children, trying to explain to them what was going on, I was struck by an event I had often noticed but on which I had never reflected. A player who failed to catch a ball thrown his way hit the ground, rolled over, and then jumped up, celebrating as though he had caught the pass after all. The referee was standing in a position that did not give him a good view of what had happened, was fooled by the player's pretense, and so moved the ball down the field. The player rushed back to the huddle so that his team could run another play before the officials had a chance to review the tape. (Until 1993, National Football League officials could watch a television replay and change their call, as long as the next play had not been run.) But viewers at home did have the benefit of the replay, and we saw what the referee missed: the ball lying on the ground instead of snug in the receiver's hands. The only comment from the broadcasters: "What a heads-up play!" Meaning: "Wow, what a great liar this kid is! Well done!"[1]

This is a story we recognize! In much of the United States, truth is defined as what allows us to get ahead. Sometimes it's little more than who screams the loudest on Ricki Lake or who appears more winsome on Larry King. James Patterson and Peter Kim put the truth of the matter rather baldly after an extensive study of

Americans' truth-telling habits: "Americans lie. They lie more than we had ever thought possible before the study."[2]

What should the response of Christ followers be? Well, we shouldn't be shocked. Our job isn't to scold our neighbors with condemnations for not telling the truth. Rather, our job is to be a countercultural community that boldly follows Jesus.

So in the area of integrity, exactly where will following in his steps take us?

WHAT JESUS TAUGHT

Jesus' most extensive teaching on honesty is in Matthew 5:33–37. This passage is the fourth of six illustrations showing how the righteousness of his followers was to be deeper than that of the Pharisees and teachers of the law:

> Again, you have heard that it was said to the people long ago, "Do not break your oath, but keep the oaths you have made to the Lord." But I tell you, Do not swear at all: either by heaven, for it is God's throne; or by the earth, for it is his footstool; or by Jerusalem, for it is the city of the Great King. And do not swear by your head, for you cannot make even one hair white or black. Simply let your "Yes" be "Yes," and your "No," "No"; anything beyond this comes from the evil one.

The people had often heard the religious experts refer to the third commandment: "You shall not misuse the name of the Lord your God." The focus of this commandment wasn't primarily on cursing but on honoring God by keeping your word. A paraphrase might be: "Honor God enough so that when you invoke his name in an oath, you carry out the promise." The teaching of the Old Testament had been crystal clear: God's people are to be aboveboard and honest—people of their word.

But to some of the Pharisees and teachers, there were a few loopholes in the third commandment. If we are told to keep our oaths made to the Lord, doesn't that open up an escape clause for other oaths—oaths not made "to the Lord"?

Apparently they were making promises that they considered less binding. These promises were made not to the Lord but to heaven, earth, Jerusalem, or even one's own head. Their escape clause is perhaps clearer in Matthew 23:16–22:

> Woe to you, blind guides! You say, "If anyone swears by the temple, it means nothing; but if anyone swears by the gold of the temple, he is bound by his oath." You blind fools! Which is greater: the gold, or the temple that makes the gold sacred? You also say, "If anyone swears by the altar, it means nothing; but if anyone swears by the gift on it, he is bound by his oath." You blind men! Which is greater: the gift, or the altar that makes the gift sacred? Therefore, he who swears by the altar swears by it and by everything on it. And he who swears by the temple swears by it and by the one who dwells in it. And he who swears by heaven swears by God's throne and by the one who sits on it.

They had adulterated the clear intent of Scripture! No matter what they swore by, it was related to God and his integrity. Heaven is his throne, while the earth is his footstool. Jerusalem is the Great King's city. And we, unlike God, can't control the destiny of even one hair on our head. (These were obviously pre-Rogaine and pre-Grecian Formula times!)

We can't miss the direct demands of Jesus' teaching. The community of faith shouldn't need to take oaths at all. It should be clear to all that our word is good. Our "yes" must mean "yes," and our "no" must mean "no."

How Jesus Lived

Throughout his life, Jesus told the truth no matter the consequences. From the earliest days when he told his parents he had to be about his Father's business to the final hours when he refused to take Pilate's bait and instead insisted that he was a king—a charge Pilate couldn't overlook—Jesus was a man of his word. He said what he meant; he meant what he said.[3]

The gospel of John forcefully underscores Jesus' intimate connection with truth. "In fact, for this reason I was born," Jesus tells Pilate, "and for this I came into the world, to testify to the truth."[4] Since he came from above, he was obligated to live and embody truth. Those who opposed him and the truth he brought were siding with Satan, who ought to be listed in *The Guinness Book of Records* for the greatest liar. Listen to Jesus describe him:

> You belong to your father, the devil, and you want to carry out your father's desire. He was a murderer from the beginning, not holding to the truth, for there is no truth in him. When he lies, he speaks his native language, for he is a liar and the father of lies. Yet because I tell the truth, you do not believe me! Can any of you prove me guilty of sin? If I am telling the truth, why don't you believe me? He who belongs to God hears what God says. The reason you do not hear is that you do not belong to God.[5]

There were many indications of his commitment to truth:

- Jesus' statements often began by saying, "I tell you the truth."[6]
- He held up God's Word, which was truth.[7]
- He left the Spirit of truth to guide his disciples.[8]

While some of his opponents accused him of widespread deception, the charge wouldn't stick.[9] Over and over this one who was the Way, the Truth, and the Life spoke more truth than they had ever heard. Real truth. Penetrating truth. "If you hold to my teaching, you are really my disciples," he told them. "Then you will know the truth, and the truth will set you free."[10]

So completely was God's Word and life embodied in Jesus that John reported years after his death: "The law was given through Moses; grace and truth came through Jesus Christ."[11]

Jesus didn't just tell the truth. His every word and action embodied truth. Doing what Jesus would do means that the Christian life embodies truth all the time, to all people, and in all situations.

Truth in John's gospel isn't just some abstract concept. It is ultimately the presence of God's redemptive work in Jesus Christ.

CHRIST FOLLOWERS IN A PINOCCHIO CULTURE

"Where he leads me I will follow," the old hymn intones. In this instance following Jesus clearly means we will be people of our word. We will avoid not only the larger-than-Jupiter lies that treat truth like Silly Putty, but also the tiny, polite, casual lies that are so commonplace:

- "The check is in the mail."
- "I thought the light was still yellow."
- "I need just a minute of your time."
- "No, you didn't wake me up."

Tom Eddins, a friend who teaches at a Christian university, has collected some of his favorite student fibs through the years. The best is from the girl who again missed his 8:00 A.M. class. She later came by his office to explain what had happened. She had reached for her alarm clock and accidentally knocked it off, causing it to fall on her head, knocking her out! Tom didn't know whether to be impressed with the ingenious story or insulted that she thought he might really buy it.

Such casual lying infects every area of life. Consider the top ten lies husbands and wives foist upon each other.

10. "I don't remember your saying that."

9. "I called to apologize, but the line was busy."

8. "I'd love to have your mother stay with us a week."

7. "It was on sale."

6. "I promise not to ask you again."

5. "I'll do it during the next commercial."

4. "I have a headache."

3. "I didn't hear you."

2. "I didn't mean to hurt your feelings."

1. "I'm almost ready."

I understand well how tempting it is to bend the truth just a few degrees. When our daughter had just turned two and our son was four, we took them to Disney World. Little did we know the difference turning two makes if you want to see Mickey Mouse. For children under two it's *free*. If they are two or older, the cost is around $8000 (not to exaggerate in a chapter on lying!).

Immediately, rationalizations filled my mind. First, I told myself that other parents with kids Megan's age were certainly not paying. Some of the kids they took through free were already shaving. The parents would just explain, "He's facially advanced."

Second, I knew that Disney wouldn't miss the money like I would. I couldn't picture a headline in the *Orlando Sentinel* that read "Goofy Laid Off: Minister Fails to Pay for Daughter!"

The most insidious rationalization, though, was when I remembered that Megan, who had been two for only a week, had been born three weeks prematurely. She really shouldn't be two yet!

Though I did pay for her after my internal debate, I remember the temptation well. It's the same temptation other Christians face when it comes to preparing a résumé, deciding whether to take a day of vacation or call in sick, turning in expense reports, or filing an income-tax return. Supposedly the IRS once received this note:

Gentlemen:

Enclosed you will find a check for $150. I cheated on my income tax return last year and have not been able to sleep ever since. If I still have trouble sleeping, I will send you the rest.

Sincerely,
John Taxpayer

"What would Jesus do?" we ask again. The Gospels are clear: He would consistently tell the truth. He would let his "yes" mean "yes."

FIB-INFESTED WATERS

Recently two people told me things that were difficult to believe. One person I didn't believe because I've come to know him as a person who hedges, fudges, and fibs. The other person I did believe, though, because I've come to know him as a man of honesty.

The church should be filled with the latter, with men and women of complete integrity. If we are to be the salt of the earth and the light of the world as Jesus said, we must rise above the fib-infested waters.

Christ following leads to truth!

Almighty and tender Lord Jesus Christ,
I have asked you to be good to my friends,
and now I bring before you what I desire in my heart for my
    enemies. . . .

[I]f what I ask for them at any time
is outside the rule of charity,
whether through weakness, ignorance, or malice,
good Lord, do not give it to them
and do not give it back to me.

You who are the light, lighten their darkness;
you who are the whole truth, correct their errors;
you who are the true life, give life to their souls. . . .

Tender Lord Jesus,
let me not be the cause of the death of my brothers,
let me not be to them
a stone of stumbling and a rock of offense.

Let them be reconciled to you and in concord with me,
according to your will and for your own sake.

Do this, my good Creator and my merciful Judge,
according to your mercy that cannot be measured.
Forgive me all my debts
as I before you forgive all those indebted to me.
Perhaps this may not be so
because in your sight I have not yet done this perfectly,
but my will is set to do it,
and to that end I am doing all I can.

I have prayed as a weak man and a sinner;
you who are mighty and merciful, hear my prayer.

St. Anselm, A prayer for his enemies

CHAPTER SEVEN

Injustice

Corrie ten Boom had seen all she could endure. The guards in her Nazi concentration camp had ridiculed her sister, Betsie, constantly. One guard over their digging crew had grabbed the tiny handful of dirt that Betsie had shoveled, all that she'd been able to lift in her frail condition, and had shown it to everyone, taunting her with biting remarks. Then the guard took a leather strip and slashed her across the chest and neck.

Flush with pure anger, Corrie grabbed a shovel and rushed at the guard. But she was interrupted by her sister, whose collar was quickly turning red from the cut. Betsie pleaded with her to keep working. She covered the whip mark Corrie was staring at and said gently but firmly, "Don't look at it, Corrie. Look at Jesus only."

Years later Corrie had a chance to remember Betsie's urgent words. After the war she was speaking in Munich on forgiveness, and after she finished a man came to her with his hand extended: "Yes, it is wonderful that Jesus forgives us all our sins, just as you say."

But the sight of his face repulsed her. Standing before her with his hand extended was one of the leering guards from the concentration camp who had degraded and humiliated her and other women as they had showered. Her hand froze, unwilling to touch him.

Horrified at both the memory and her inability to forgive, she prayed, "Lord, forgive me. I cannot forgive." Immediately, as she confessed her need for forgiveness, her hand loosened. The freezing chill of hatred thawed. She embraced the former guard, forgiving him as she herself had been forgiven in Jesus Christ.

These powerful scenes stir us decades later as we hear again Betsie's plea: *Look at Jesus only.* But as we hear her words, we can't help but see some faces ourselves.

Some see the faces of people who inflicted pain on them. Perhaps it was the pain of an abusive relationship or a crime. It could be the physical or emotional whelps that came from bigots who in their small-minded, anger-filled world made race a weapon. Some remember walking away from the cemetery where their child was buried only to later see the drunk driver walk away from the courts unscathed.

Others picture faces of people who neglected them—maybe parents who were so busy trying to maintain a certain lifestyle that they forgot to maintain a life.

For some, these faces belong to people who abandoned them. One woman I know put her husband through professional school, gave birth to three kids, tried to hold all their worlds together, and then learned that he was leaving her for someone else. He said he never really loved her.

Others recall well the faces of those who damaged their reputation by lying about them, by prejudging them, by claiming to know their motives. I think back to the time a friend of ours visited a small church while on vacation with his family—only to hear a vicious sermon attacking *him*. The minister, a pit bull for Christ who certainly didn't know his target was in the audience that morning, had never met or even corresponded with him.

Injustice stings. It blisters. Just months after my daughter died, an influential person in our church mailed a letter to all our elders, demanding that I be fired because of my motives (which he claimed to know to be evil). This scud missile, launched without my awareness by a person who had helped convince me to move to the church a few years earlier, hit me at an emotionally vulnerable time. Though my church leaders supported me completely, week after week I continued preaching with this person in clear view.

You've been there, haven't you? Different circumstances, but similar story.

So what do we do with this injustice? I know of only three possibilities.

1. *We can try to ignore it.* Sweep it under the rug and forget about it. Unfortunately, however, this doesn't work. The bump under the rug keeps getting bigger. Eventually it consumes the whole room. Then we suffocate.

2. *We can try to retaliate.* Punch back. Flash your headlights back. Throw a party and don't invite them. Cut off all communication. Circulate gossip. Get her fired. Honk your horn.

Part of why *Unforgiven* (1992) and *Braveheart* (1995) received Academy Awards for Best Picture was that so many could identify with the desire to get even. Who could stand to live with an uneven score? This simple rhyme by W. H. Auden reflects the world's standard:

> I and the public know
> What all school children learn—

Those to whom evil is done
Do evil in return.

But retaliation doesn't get us anywhere. "Eye-for-eye" just leaves everyone with swollen eyes and pints of dripping blood. Each time we pay back evil for evil, we're just feeding coins to the Evil Machine, guaranteeing that it continues playing.

3. *We can forgive.* The third possibility is the only one open to those who are serious about following Jesus Christ. It is the miracle-working gift of forgiveness.

WHAT JESUS TAUGHT

"You have heard that it was said, 'Eye for eye, and tooth for tooth,'" Jesus said to his disciples. Not only is eye-for-eye the way of the world, it was the way preached by some of the religious leaders. And in this instance, they were armed with the heavy artillery of biblical texts. (Nothing is more dangerous than religious zealots who have texts lined up like semiautomatic weapons!) For example, Deuteronomy had instructed Israel to "show no pity: life for life, eye for eye, tooth for tooth, hand for hand, foot for foot."[1]

Jesus knew these Bible scholars had missed some vital things about these texts. First, the passages provided punishment that would be determined by courts not by vigilantes out to even a score. And second, they actually provided some protection by limiting the amount of punishment that could be meted out. They couldn't, for example, pay back "head for arm" as human tendency might prefer.

Jesus took people back to God's true intentions, which had little to do with retaliation:

> But I tell you, Do not resist an evil person. If someone strikes you on the right cheek, turn to him the other also. And if someone wants to sue you and take your tunic, let

him have your cloak as well. If someone forces you to go one mile, go with him two miles. Give to the one who asks you, and do not turn away from the one who wants to borrow from you.[2]

Jesus tells us to respond to evil with love, match insult with blessing, offer smiles in exchange for scowls, and give forgiveness in the place of bitterness. We are to be part of a reconciling community where broken bones of division are healed, where hostility is defused, and where gaps of hurt are bridged.

Can you imagine the restorative potential for rush-hour traffic, for long lines at the grocery store, for feuding families, for racial walls, and for congregational division?

Then Jesus continues:

You have heard that it was said, "Love your neighbor and hate your enemy." But I tell you: Love your enemies and pray for those who persecute you, that you may be sons of your Father in heaven. He causes his sun to rise on the evil and the good, and sends rain on the righteous and the unrighteous. If you love those who love you, what reward will you get? Are not even the tax collectors doing that? And if you greet only your brothers, what are you doing more than others? Do not even pagans do that? Be perfect, therefore, as your heavenly Father is perfect.[3]

Every good Pharisee knew that God had commanded them to "love your neighbor as yourself."[4] But some had assumed that if they were to love their neighbors—interpreted to mean "all us good folks"—then the flip side of the coin must also be true: God wants us to hate our enemies. So in a roundabout way, they could be fully faithful to God's law only by despising people like the half-breed Samaritans, the turncoat tax collectors, and the Romans who were occupying their land.

"Righteous hatred" is a tailored suit that always seems to fit! It allows you to reserve your compassionate and loving behavior for those who like you, while unleashing your bitterness on your enemies. This might include:

- a sibling who drained all the family's emotional energy or all the family's financial resources so there were none left for you

- a competitor whose idea of fair advertising includes hype and lies so that now you're suffering

- a teacher, a church leader, a spouse, a former spouse, a boss—all those who have made it their job to make your life miserable

"Righteous hatred" is a high-octane fuel that burns forever as churchgoers lash out viciously at politicians, educators, media, and anyone else considered to be *the enemy*.

But Jesus' words lead us down another road. He insists not only that we refrain from paying back eye-for-eye to our enemy but also that we engage in loving actions toward him. We are to love with a *one-way love*. One-way love is unmotivated (except by God's love for us), nonselective, and unilateral. We are to love as God loves. He sends his rain on the just and the unjust.

Frederick Buechner put it eloquently in *The Magnificent Defeat*:

The love for equals is a human thing . . . of friend for friend, brother for brother. It is to love what is loving and lovely. The world smiles.

The love for the less fortunate is a beautiful thing . . . the love for those who suffer, for those who are poor, the sick, the misfits, the failures, the unlovely. This love is heartfelt compassion, and it touches the heart of the world.

The love for the more fortunate is a rare thing . . . to love those who succeed where we fail, to rejoice without envy with those who rejoice, the love of the poor for the rich, of the black man for the white man. The world is bewildered by its saints.

And then there is the love for the enemy . . . love for the one who does not love you but rather who mocks, threatens, and inflicts pain. The tortured's love for the torturer. This is God's love. And it conquers the world.[5]

What can we do about the injustices we've suffered? How do we respond when others have lied about us, hurt our children, or treated us unfairly? The answer Jesus offers is forgiveness.

"Lord, how many times shall I forgive my brother when he sins against me? Up to seven times?" Peter, with his own version of "three strikes and you're out," asked him magnanimously.

Jesus replied, "I tell you, not seven times, but seventy-seven times."[6] Then he told this story:

> The kingdom of heaven is like a king who wanted to settle accounts with his servants. As he began the settlement, a man who owed him ten thousand talents was brought to him. Since he was not able to pay, the master ordered that he and his wife and his children and all that he had be sold to repay the debt.
>
> The servant fell on his knees before him. "Be patient with me," he begged, "and I will pay back everything." The servant's master took pity on him, canceled the debt and let him go.
>
> But when that servant went out, he found one of his fellow servants who owed him a hundred denarii. He grabbed him and began to choke him. "Pay back what you owe me!" he demanded.
>
> His fellow servant fell to his knees and begged him, "Be patient with me, and I will pay you back."
>
> But he refused. Instead, he went off and had the man thrown into prison until he could pay the debt. When the other servants saw what had happened, they were greatly

distressed and went and told their master everything that had happened.

Then the master called the servant in. "You wicked servant," he said, "I canceled all that debt of yours because you begged me to. Shouldn't you have had mercy on your fellow servant just as I had on you?" In anger his master turned him over to the jailers to be tortured, until he should pay back all he owed.[7]

Step one in offering forgiveness to those who have been unjust is to realize that there is darkness in *you*. You have contributed to the brokenness of the world. Understand your own capacity for evil and your own need for costly grace. Otherwise, your quest to forgive others will be condescending and trite. It will be full of victimizing language.

Christianity offers this foundational truth: You forgive not because it will heal you and not because you're so loving but because you have received forgiveness from God. You forgive others because "in Christ God forgave you."[8]

Imagine a woman trying to forgive her husband who has abandoned her and their children for another woman. She'll probably have to endure the thoughtless words of a few amateur counselors who insist that "there are always two sides to the story." No, not always. In this instance, he was wrong. He let his hormones win over his vow. But she forgives the man who walked out on her not because she owes it to him or because he asked for it, but because God forgave her!

Forgiving him doesn't mean that she'll forget what happened. The hard drives in our skulls don't erase easily. Nor does it imply that she must repress her feelings. She will likely need an opportunity to express her anger so the anger doesn't petrify into bitterness. And it certainly doesn't mean she should tolerate the evil. She would not allow him to stay at home and pretend everything is normal while continuing the affair, for example.

Forgiveness does signify her willingness to cut him free from the harm he's brought. It means she is courageously willing to live with an uneven score, to resist retaliation, to treat him lovingly (even if she doesn't feel particularly loving), to pray for him, and to turn his future over to God.

"Forgive us our debts," Jesus taught us to pray, "as we also have forgiven our debtors."[9]

How Jesus Lived

Did Jesus' life match his words? How did he respond when faced with injustice? There could be no better model to follow because no one has ever been treated more unfairly, and no one has ever responded with a more forgiving spirit.

One time, for example, Jesus ran up against the accumulated racial tension of many years. The people of a Samaritan village, knowing he was on his way to Jerusalem, refused to welcome him.[10] James and John didn't take the insult well. "Lord," they seethed with steam rising from their foreheads, "do you want us to call fire down from heaven to destroy them?"

Jesus surely disarmed them by directing his rebuke to them rather than to the villagers. Retaliation just wasn't his style.

The clearest example of his forgiving spirit, of course, was the cross. "The cross is the only power in the world," wrote Dietrich Bonhoeffer, "which proves that suffering love can avenge and vanquish evil."

The charges hurled against Jesus were trumped up and false. He was accused of evil while he came only for good. The prophet Isaiah had anticipated the injustice of his punishment centuries before:

> Surely he took up our infirmities
>   and carried our sorrows,
> yet we considered him stricken by God,
>   smitten by him, and afflicted.

But he was pierced for our transgressions,
   he was crushed for our iniquities;
the punishment that brought us peace was upon him,
   and by his wounds we are healed.[11]

In the face of sheer hatred, Jesus prayed, "Father, forgive them, for they do not know what they are doing."[12] The apostle Peter would later call on Christians to refrain from retaliation because of their model, Jesus Christ:

To this you were called, because Christ suffered for you, leaving you an example, that you should follow in his steps. "He committed no sin, and no deceit was found in his mouth." When they hurled their insults at him, he did not retaliate; when he suffered, he made no threats. Instead, he entrusted himself to him who judges justly.[13]

It was a lesson Peter had learned personally. After disowning Jesus three times, what hope could he possibly have had that Jesus would forgive him and use him again to bring people to God? But even before his denial, Jesus, fully aware of what would happen, extended mercy: "Simon, Simon, Satan has asked to sift you as wheat. But I have prayed for you, Simon, that your faith may not fail. And when you have turned back, strengthen your brothers."[14]

ESCAPING CRUEL UNFAIRNESS

No aspect of imitating Jesus will take more trust in his guidance than this one. There is a reason the world lives by revenge: It is extremely satisfying. It is a lifesaver that you can roll around in your mouth and savor. It is living by the bumper-sticker motto: *I don't get mad. I get even.* But beware: It is laced with poison!

So, is it even possible to answer injustice with forgiveness? Listen to this courageous response from one young Christ follower, a university student who wrote me about an unthinkable cruelty in her life:

In my ordeal of trying so desperately to forgive them, I opened my heart to God and allowed him to help me. . . . God tells us that if we keep on knocking, the door will be opened. It took me a while even to knock, but once I did, and kept at it, the door [of forgiveness] was opened.

I still struggle daily with negative feelings and many overwhelming needs for forgiveness in many areas of my life, as we all do. It is a constant task of knocking, and each day I learn that God has many blessings stored up for me.

Four years after the worst experience in my life, I can honestly say that I do forgive the two men who raped me. I discovered in forgiving them that I am not a bad person because of what was done to me. I replaced anger with forgiveness and hate with compassion. Often I am frightened at night in the dark, but it is at these times that I allow myself to fall asleep with the light on. Being sure not to give in to my fear of the dark, I first open my Bible and read Colossians 3:13, "Bear with each other and forgive whatever grievances you may have against one another. Forgive as the Lord forgave you."

Closing my Bible I am convinced that we need to forgive those who sin against us. It is comforting to know that God's exact Word is being applied to my life.

How had this young believer found the courage to stop the hellish cycle of pain? By keeping her eyes on Jesus Christ! She had learned the secret. Forgiveness is the blood that reoxygenates our weary bodies and souls; the mortar that holds our houses and homes together; and the North Star that keeps our lives and relationships on course.

OUR ONLY PASSAGE

The footsteps of Jesus are leading us in a bold new direction. Not many will choose to follow. They lead away from revenge to mercy. Away from bitterness to forgiveness. While it's not a well-traveled path, it is the one that leads to freedom!

Our only escape from history's cruel unfairness, our only passage to the future's creative possibilities, is the miracle of forgiving.[15]

Yes, we need a renewed awareness of death. But we need far more. We need a faith, in the midst of our groanings, that death is not the last word, but the next to last. What is mortal will be swallowed up by life. One day all whispers of death will fall silent.

Philip Yancey, Christianity Today

CHAPTER EIGHT

Death

In John Updike's fourth and final novel about Harry "Rabbit" Angstrom, Harry dwells on the bleakness of his late middle age. Harry is a local basketball star turned Toyota distributor, through whom Updike scrutinizes four decades of American culture. Harry is consumed by thoughts of impending death—thoughts fed by the crash of Pan Am flight 747 over Lockerbie, Scotland.

As he dwells on "those bodies tumbling down like wet melon seeds," he fears his own approaching end. In an ICU room after a heart attack, Harry realizes that his obsession with the wreck isn't so much about the victims as about himself:

107

> He too is falling, helplessly falling, toward death. The fate awaiting him behind this veil of medical attention is as absolute as that which greeted those bodies fallen smack upon the boggy Scottish earth like garbage bags full of water. Smack, splat, bodies bursting across the golf courses and heathery lanes of Lockerbie drenched in night. What met them was no more than what awaits him. Reality broke upon those passengers as they sat carving their airline chicken with the unwrapped silver or dozing with tubes piping Barry Manilow into their ears and that same icy black reality has broken upon him; death is not a domesticated pet of life but a beast that . . . will swallow him, it is truly there under him, vast as a planet at night, gigantic and totally his. His death. The burning intensifies in his sore throat and he feels all but suffocated by terror.[1]

Harry isn't the only one with such inner terror over death. Aging generation after aging generation has dwelt upon the implications of the certain end of life. Because of the deep and dark appearance of death, it is often pictured as a river. In Greek mythology, for example, it was the River Styx, a dreary, poisonous river, that ran between earth and hades. The one crossing would have to pay a fee to Charon, the boatman who ferried people across.

In John Bunyan's *The Pilgrim's Progress*, Christian and Hopeful come to the Celestial City in the land of Beulah. But between them and the glorious city is a deep, scary river through which everyone must pass.

> Now I further saw, that betwixt them and the gate was a river; but there was no bridge to go over, and the river was very deep. At the sight, therefore, of this river, the pilgrims were much stunned; but the men that went with them said, "You must go through, or you cannot come at the gate."

. . . The pilgrims then, especially Christian, began to despond in his mind, and looked this way and that; but no way could be found by them by which they might escape the river.[2]

Even an old spiritual said, "I have one more river to cross. My brother, my sister, my father, my mother—they'll all be waiting, but they can't help me across."

There is a question lurking behind this fear of the river of death: Is death a transition or a final statement? Is it a period or a comma? This is the question that bothers humans all of their lives. Everything is either dead or dying. When I turned forty, many of my closest friends gathered to throw a surprise party. How nice to have the people you love the most remind you that you're on the downhill slide toward death!

Can't you identify with the concerns about death? Have you buried a parent or a best friend and felt the chill blow over the river? Have you sat up all night listening to pumps and watching air being taken in with great difficulty? Have you maybe flirted with the river with one of your own children? Do you still remember the exact location of the hands on the clock when the call came from the hospital?

Where can we turn but to the Lord whom we are following? The writer of Hebrews tied the human existence of Jesus to our fear of death: "Since the children have flesh and blood, he too shared in their humanity so that by his death he might destroy him who holds the power of death—that is, the devil—and free those who all their lives were held in slavery by their fear of death."[3] There is a new path to navigate the waters of death. Jesus is the compass!

WHAT JESUS TAUGHT

A first-time reader of the Gospels, approaching the text with the existential questions of our age, might be struck by how seldom Jesus spoke about death. We might have supposed that he would concentrate his teaching on that area of human concern, but he didn't.

At times Jesus related death to the life we are called upon to live as we follow him. Life in Christ isn't about "grabbing all the gusto," but about pouring out our lives as a sacrifice for others.

He then began to teach them that the Son of Man must suffer many things and be rejected by the elders, chief priests, and teachers of the law, and that he must be killed and after three days rise again. He spoke plainly about this, and Peter took him aside and began to rebuke him.

But when Jesus turned and looked at his disciples, he rebuked Peter. "Get behind me, Satan!" he said. "You do not have in mind the things of God, but the things of men."

Then he called the crowd to him along with his disciples and said: "If anyone would come after me, he must deny himself and take up his cross and follow me. For whoever wants to save his life will lose it, but whoever loses his life for me and for the gospel will save it. What good is it for a man to gain the whole world, yet forfeit his soul? Or what can a man give in exchange for his soul?"[4]

Juan Carlos Ortiz says that often in Argentina when someone is baptized, the person performing the baptism will say, "I kill you in the name of the Father, the Son, and the Holy Spirit."[5] How appropriate! Following Jesus means that we no longer live for selfish interests. We are now consumed by passion for the interests of the kingdom of God. Death is a teaching aid in pointing us to kingdom life! Furthermore, death doesn't have to be feared. "Do not be afraid of those who kill the body but cannot kill the soul," Jesus told his disciples.[6]

It would be a terrible tragedy to be lost eternally; physical death, on the other hand, isn't so terrifying. It is a necessary transition to the place Jesus has prepared for his followers.[7]

When he predicted his own death with the ominous words "the hour has come," Jesus pointed to the role of death in nature:

I tell you the truth, unless a kernel of wheat falls to the ground and dies, it remains only a single seed. But if it dies, it produces many seeds. The man who loves his life will lose it, while the man who hates his life in this world will keep it for eternal life.[8]

This isn't to say, however, that Jesus considered death to be "normal." Any time he saw a funeral, he winced. The one who came to bring abundant life was offended by the pain and loss that death brought. The kingdom was breaking forth through the power of his life and word to reverse that. When John the Baptist inquired about his ministry, Jesus pointed to this great reversal: "The blind receive sight, the lame walk, those who have leprosy are cured, the deaf hear, the dead are raised, and the good news is preached to the poor."[9]

Of course, not all the blind, lame, leprous, and deaf were healed. Certainly not all the dead were raised. But still, an inexorable reversal had begun. The kingdom, which will be consummated only when the Lord returns, had taken a firm hold.

Diane Komp is a pediatric oncologist whose books tell of her struggle for faith amid hurting and dying children. I can assure you from experience: Pediatric hospitals are a difficult place for light, breezy faith. Yet on the other hand, they are good places to find rugged, real-life faith.

Komp tells about a woman who became almost as close as a sister to her. This woman's six-year-old son never really responded to treatment—he had little chance of living.

Day after day, Sammy's mother sat with him, often playing Christian music. Komp describes the dark circumstances of the room that Sammy shared with three others:

> He was in a room with three other brain-damaged boys, worse off than he, if such was possible. One child had fallen out of a fourth-story window. Another had been beaten. The third was the hapless victim of a hit-and-run driver. The room was a vegetable garden, filled with

wilting young life. Mothers sat patiently at their sons' sides, encouraging them with their therapy, hoping and praying for a miracle.

One day as Komp visited with Sammy's mom, they were interrupted by his music—which he had turned up full blast. He wanted to hear and for others to hear the triumphant words: "We declare that the kingdom of God is here! The blind see, the deaf hear, the lame men are walking. Sicknesses flee at his voice. The dead live again, and the poor hear the good news. Jesus is King, so rejoice!"

When the song finished, he hit the rewind button and played it loudly again. Komp asked him, "You really believe that, don't you, kiddo?" It was clear that he believed it. The question she had to ask was, *Did she believe it?*[10]

This is the mystery of Jesus' coming: The kingdom of God has broken it. It has broken the power of sin and death and has initiated a process that will only come to full fruition when he returns.

HOW JESUS LIVED

Perhaps Jesus' perspective on death can best be seen through three times when he met death face to face. One time was when a synagogue ruler named Jairus came desperately seeking his help. "My little daughter is dying. Please come and put your hands on her so that she will be healed and live."[11] Mark reports Jesus' answer very simply: "So Jesus went with him." Imagine that! Thousands of people around, each with a different set of pressing needs. Yet the urgent plea of this father touched him so deeply that he went.

By the time he reached Jairus's home, it was too late. At least, that's how it seemed to everyone. For the twelve-year-old was dead. Relatives and friends were crying out loudly. Yet Jesus insisted that she wasn't dead but sleeping, for the Lord of Life was in their midst!

He took the girl's lifeless hand and commanded, "Little girl, I say to you, get up!" And at his word, she stood up and began walking around. Mark adds, as if we wouldn't have imagined it anyway, "At this they were completely astonished."

Did he save her from death? Well, yes and no. He brought her back from death at that moment. Still, eventually (Wouldn't we imagine decades later?) she died. But this was an opportunity for taking on death—with all of the pain and offense to God's life it brings.

Another time, Jesus was entering the small village of Nain when he bumped into a funeral procession.[12] The dead person was the only son of the heartbroken mother. Luke adds, because it pointed to her helpless situation, that she was a widow.

Jesus' response was of undiluted compassion. This was not the kind of "man on a mission" who often fails to see the frowns and tears of those around him. He told her not to cry and then touched the coffin. Jesus commanded, "Young man, I say to you, get up!" Immediately the man sat up and started talking.

Again, we have to remember that Jesus didn't ultimately deliver this man from death—just death at that time. But he responded to the grief of the mother just as he had responded to the dire plea of Jairus. In both cases, he had a chance to taunt death.

A third time Jesus faced death was when his friend Lazarus died. The man's sisters, Mary and Martha, had sent word to him that he was needed in Bethany ASAP because Lazarus was ill. But by the time he got there, it seemed too late. When he arrived, there was a dismal spirit in the air. Both sisters were upset that he hadn't come the moment he found out about Lazarus's sickness.

> "Lord," Martha said to Jesus, "if you had been here, my brother would not have died. But I know that even now God will give you whatever you ask." Jesus said to her, "Your brother will rise again." Martha answered, "I know he will rise again in the resurrection at the last day."[13]

But how will that happen? How do we know there is an answer for the endless procession of hearses? Jesus replies, "I am the resurrection and the life. He who believes in me will live, even though he dies; and whoever lives and believes in me will never die."

Throughout the gospel of John, Jesus is revealed as the giver of life: a life that is anchored in the knowledge of God through Jesus and that is lived here and now.[14] But at this scene of mourning he reveals that even death cannot take this life away. It is a life that will conquer the grave! One of his followers would celebrate this victory in these words: "I am convinced that neither death nor life, neither angels nor demons, neither the present nor the future, nor any powers, neither height nor depth, nor anything else in all creation, will be able to separate us from the love of God that is in Christ Jesus our Lord."[15]

Then Jesus asked Martha the critical question: "Do you believe this?" It's a question that seems overworked—even trite—when asked in a seminary or even in a Sunday school class. But for those standing on the edge of "the River," it is the most important question in life. Does he have the power over death or doesn't he?

FREED FROM FEAR

As a minister, I have had the opportunity to help people confront questions about death many times. Like many others, I've stood over the fresh grave sites of ninety-year-old great-grandmothers and of newborn infants. A few times I've had to escort friends or police to homes to inform people of tragic, unexpected deaths. And many times, I've sat in hospital rooms with older people who know that the end is inevitable.

But I've faced these questions not just as a minister. I've also faced them as a grieving father. From that day at 10:16 A.M. when my daughter died, I've been faced personally with my beliefs. Is this just something good to preach because it helps people deal with life? Or is it bedrock truth?

Most of us can probably identify with Woody Allen: "I don't mind dying. I just don't want to be there when it happens." It's great to talk about life. But when we look in the mirror and see wrinkles and receding hairlines or when we look in the obit column and see familiar names or look at old family slides and remember how many are now missing, we are faced with several possible fears:

1. *The fear of loneliness.* At that moment, will we feel all alone—since no one can exactly die with us?

2. *The fear of the unknown.* Who, despite all of the "been there, done that, came back to tell about it" books, really knows what the moments of dying are really like?

3. *The fear of being forgotten.* Will we be just another brief blip on the map of life that is quickly gone and ignored?

But those of us who follow Jesus Christ realize that he, the Resurrection and the Life, has yanked the sting out of the scorpion of death.[16] We may not know the answers to all the mysteries of death, but we do know that Jesus has conquered death and that we do not have to experience it alone. He who was crucified and raised has promised to be with us at all times. This impacts us in at least three ways.

First, it impacts the way we grieve. It takes us to the gravesides of parents, children, and friends and reminds us that Act II of God's drama still remains. This second act has already been written; it just hasn't been performed. In our grief, we now remember that God will transform their bodies. The lame will walk. The deaf will hear. The blind will see. Those with Alzheimer's will remember, and the cancerous will be cancer-free.

Actually, walking, hearing, seeing, and remembering are merely limited representations of what the ultimate healing of transformation might encompass. But as we grieve now, we shed both tears of sadness and tears of joyful anticipation.

Second, it impacts the way we live. Our belief in Jesus as the Resurrection and the Life impacts the way we live. Because of God's work through his Deliverer, we can be fully devoted to something that will last on the other side of the grave. Money will be passed on. Houses will eventually be destroyed. But heavenly investments will yield eternal interest!

Third, it impacts the way we approach our own deaths. Just as there is a Christian lifestyle, there must be a Christian deathstyle. The old spiritual said that none of the people I know—mother, father, brother, sister—can usher me across the river of death safely. But it continues: "My Jesus, he'll be a' waitin' there, And he can help me across."

Likewise, Bunyan's story about Christian and Hopeful continues:

> Then they asked the men if the waters were all of a depth. They said, "No . . . you shall find it deeper or shallower as you believe in the King of the place."
>
> They then addressed themselves to the water; and, entering, Christian began to sink, and crying out to his good friend Hopeful, he said, "I sink in deep waters; the billows go over my head; all His waves go over me."
>
> Then said the other, "Be of good cheer, my brother; I feel the bottom, and it is good."
>
> . . . And, with that, Christian brake out with a loud voice, "Oh, I see Him again; and He tells me, 'When thou passest through the waters, I will be with thee; and through the rivers, they shall not overflow thee.'"
>
> Then they both took courage. . . . Thus they got over.[17]

This book is about following Jesus wherever he leads. And the critical point here is that his path encompasses even death. We can follow him throughout our lives with the same view of death he had. Then, when we walk through the valley of the shadow of death, we can fear no evil, for he will be with us!

THE CHRISTIAN DEATHSTYLE

Brennan Manning was home one evening when a woman came to his door. She said her father was dying and he wanted to see a minister or priest, but she'd been unable to find anyone who could go visit him. Could he come? she wanted to know.

When Manning walked into the old man's room, he started to sit on a chair by his bed, but was quickly waved around to the other side. The man said that before he died he needed to get someone's opinion. Earlier in his life he had great difficulty praying. Someone had told him to put a chair next to him, to imagine Jesus in the chair, and to just converse with him.

He asked Manning, "Do you think Jesus minds that I do this?" explaining that at times on his deathbed he would pray toward the empty chair for an hour or two. Manning assured him that God would be happy that he'd been able to speak in prayer with greater ease.

Shortly after this Manning heard from the daughter again. She called to say that her father had died. Then before hanging up she mentioned something strange: When she walked into the room just after his last breath, she found his body twisted around so that his head was lying on that empty chair he always kept.

This belief that Jesus, the Resurrection and Life, has conquered death explains a lot about John Lee Dykes, a gentle Christ follower and a leader at the College Church in Searcy, Arkansas.

At age eighty-four, when he was diagnosed as having a rapid-spreading cancer, he and his wife, Gertrude, asked the church to pray for "his release"—not healing, but death. On June 18, 1989, he woke up twice in his sleep between 1 A.M. and 3 A.M., both times saying clearly, "I want to go home." And at 4 A.M., he died.

An odd request—to go ahead and die—cannot be fathomed by the world. But John Lee Dykes believed that what God had begun in the resurrection of Jesus Christ he would complete in the raising and transforming of his body. He believed that his wonderful Savior, who had never forsaken him, would not forsake him in the moment of death.

What a powerful testimony such a deathstyle is to unbelievers. We never exactly make a close friendship with death, but at least we don't have to live in crippling fear because of it.

Our greatest desire is to be with Jesus Christ. And in death, that quest is accomplished.

"For to me, to live is Christ and to die is gain. . . . I desire to depart and be with Christ, which is better by far."[18]

What then is permanent? What do I have that is mine forever? Of what can it be said, this will not be lost or taken away? My answer is: the promise of God to be with us always. That is the one thing which the brevity and impermanence of life will not take away.

Gene Zimmerman, *Why Do Mullets Jump?*

Poverty

Professor Robert Wuthnow of Princeton has written a book that raises some provocative questions for Christians about the relation of faith, work, and money. *God and Mammon in America* draws from a three-year national survey of 2,013 employed Americans and some in-depth interviews with a large sample of those surveyed. The survey reveals a fundamental ambivalence toward materialism among people who believe in God.

In its review of the book, *Time* summarized its central theme as "Americans are spiritually adrift when it comes to making decisions in the realm of personal economics." And the church isn't helping them, for "religion has become nothing more than a source of psychological uplifting, a tool of therapy that buttresses individual choice and lets people feel good about whatever code of conduct they choose. The ironic result, Wuthnow notes, is that those who describe themselves as committed churchgoers often have their materialistic and workaholic tendencies reinforced by their beliefs."[1]

This confusion is further illustrated by the results of a survey of employed persons conducted by the project on Religion and Economic Values at Princeton University.

71% – Being greedy is a sin against God.

84% – I wish I had more money than I do.

51% – The Bible contains valuable teachings about the use of money.

68% – Money is one thing; morals and values are completely separate.

74% – Materialism is a serious social problem.

78% – Having a beautiful home, a new car, and other nice things is "very important" or "fairly important."

Much of the biblical view of wealth is summarized by an Old Testament prophet, Jeremiah. He rebuked Jehoiakim, son of King Josiah. Josiah had been the last king of Judah who had attempted to honor Yahweh with spiritual reforms in the nation, but his sons (including King Jehoiakim) had not followed his example. Instead, this evil man had pursued personal extravagance and had used slave labor to increase his wealth. Speaking for the Lord, here is what Jeremiah told Jehoiakim:

"Woe to him who builds his palace by unrighteousness,
    his upper rooms by injustice,
making his countrymen work for nothing,
    not paying them for their labor.
He says, 'I will build myself a great palace
    with spacious upper rooms.'

So he makes large windows in it,
    panels it with cedar
    and decorates it in red.
"Does it make you a king
    to have more and more cedar?
Did not your father have food and drink?
    He did what was right and just,
    so all went well with him.
He defended the cause of the poor and needy,
    and so all went well.
Is that not what it means to know me?"
    declares the Lord.
"But your eyes and your heart
    are set only on dishonest gain,
on shedding innocent blood
    and on oppression and extortion."[2]

The italicized portion of the above passage is particularly important. Everyone who has read the Bible even casually knows that the expression "to know God" occurs frequently and expresses a central concept of genuine faith. But how can we learn to understand the expression? It clearly means more than knowing some facts about God. It has more to do with a relationship than with merely gathering information. And the ultimate means of establishing a relationship with God is, of course, through Jesus Christ. Even so, this text makes it clear that knowing God involves sharing his concern for the poor. To "defend the cause of the poor and needy" is at the heart of it. "Is that not what it means to know me?" asked Yahweh of the king who had not only been ignoring but also exploiting the poor.

Oseola McCarty of Hattiesburg, Mississippi, made national headlines by donating $150,000 to the University of Southern Mississippi to provide scholarships for African-American students. Others have made larger gifts to schools in terms of the dollars involved. What made her gift newsworthy is that she earned that money from more than seventy-five years of washing other people's clothes. It represented most of her life savings. It reminded me of what Jesus said about another woman in his own time: "All these people gave their gifts out of their wealth; but she out of her poverty put in all she had to live on."[3]

Writing about sin or stress or confusion is almost natural for me, for I know about all of them from experience. I cannot write about poverty with similar familiarity. I am one of the fortunate people in the world who lives in America and experiences many of its benefits. I eat well, live in safe and rodent-free housing, and have never heard violent gunfire in my neighborhood. I drive a nice car, dress warmly in the winter, and have health insurance. I have been continuously employed for years and have all my physical needs and most of my wants satisfied.

Maybe the facts I have just shared have combined to force me to write on this subject. I have been insensitive to the poor in many situations. It has been too easy for me to forget that there are children going to bed hungry every night and adults who are sick because they lack the most basic medical care. Over the past several years, the Holy Spirit has created a deepening conviction in my heart about these situations.

On May 4, 1996, I spent an afternoon in a small village in Croatia. Thirty-six of the forty-two homes there had been destroyed by Serb soldiers who had held the area for the almost four years of fighting that followed the breaking of what was once Yugoslavia. As they evacuated Slunjska Selnica, the soldiers became mere outlaws. They tore off roofs, smashed or removed all the doors and windows, ripped out plumbing fixtures and pipes, and took away every piece of furniture. They even pulled the electrical wiring from the walls. The village still had no electricity or running water—months after the fighting had ended. I visited with one couple that was living in the hay shed of what had been their dairy barn. It was in better shape for habitation than their vandalized house.

Walking through the devastation and poverty that followed on the heels of war, a couple in their late seventies insisted that I come into their house. Having learned that I had had something to do with sending to their village a container that had food, garden seed, and wheelbarrows for them and their neighbors, they wanted to show their gratitude and tell part of their story. So a Croatian guide named Dragica, Joy Crouch, and I entered their house.

With no water, they apologized that they could not make coffee. They set what they had before us: some sugar wafers and a bottled drink. They had nothing and insisted on taking care of guests. I have so much and can be so blind to the needs of others. Father, forgive me!

How Jesus Lived

Jesus knew about poverty in a way that I do not. He didn't just visit a scene of military invasion, occupation, and cruelty. He lived in Roman-occupied territory for his entire life. Jesus didn't just witness poverty. He embraced it by choosing from heaven to be born into a peasant family.

When Joseph traveled to Bethlehem with his wife, the couple was unable to find lodging. Sure, the town was crowded with others who were there for the census. Then as now, however, the people with money could always find a place to stay. The best Mary and Joseph could find with their resources (or lack of resources) was an animal shelter. Mary's first child, a son she and Joseph named Yeshua (Jesus), was born there.[4]

Even before Jesus was born, Mary tied his coming to the poor. In her beautiful song to the Lord at Elizabeth's house, she praised Jesus for being "mindful of the humble state of his servant."[5] Beyond the implications of this pregnancy for herself, however, she saw a much larger meaning. "[Yahweh] has brought down rulers from their thrones but has lifted up the humble. He has filled the hungry with good things but has sent the rich away empty."[6] This song reflects the prophetic theme from the Old Testament that the poor often suffer at the hands of exploitive rich persons (i.e., landowners, etc.) and that part of the Messiah's work will be to bring about justice for the mistreated poor. The work of Jesus Christ is supposed to have social implications.

That Jesus knows the plight of the poor from experience is evident from the Gospels. When Joseph and Mary carried the forty-day-old child to Jerusalem for Mary's purification, they brought two birds to sacrifice on the altar.[7] Only the poorest of Israelites who could not afford a lamb were allowed to do this.[8] Since they knew the identity of the baby, surely they would have desired a lamb to sacrifice, yet their poverty made that impossible.

Jesus' public ministry began when he was baptized by John, and John was adamant about the implications of righteousness for social justice. For example, there is a general maxim about spirituality that John taught everyone who came to be baptized by him: "The man with two tunics should share with him who has none, and the one who has food should do the same."[9] That Jesus submitted to John's baptism was an endorsement of what John had been saying about this matter.

The entire time of Jesus among humankind was lived in poverty:

- He never owned a home.[10]
- Christ and his disciples took advantage of provisions in the Law of Moses for poor people.[11]
- He seems to have had to go to special lengths to pay the half-shekel temple tax.[12]
- His ministry was supported by the generosity of people who believed in him.[13]

WHAT JESUS TAUGHT

It is impossible to ignore Jesus' attention to the poor in his recorded words. In explaining the nature and purpose of his ministry, he affirmed his commitment to the poor, sick, and rejected. In Jesus' hometown of Nazareth, he was permitted to choose a section from the prophet Isaiah to read to the synagogue. This is the text he chose:

> The Spirit of the Lord is on me,
>> because he has anointed me
>> to preach good news to the poor.
> He has sent me to proclaim freedom for the prisoners
>> and recovery of sight for the blind,
>> to release the oppressed,
>> to proclaim the year of the Lord's favor.[14]

When Christ had finished reading, he said, "Today this scripture is fulfilled in your hearing." The passionate commitment to the poor that Mary anticipated in her song was thus embraced by Jesus in the earliest days of his work.

The "year of the Lord's favor" mentioned in this Isaiah passage is a reference to Jubilee.[15] The Israelites were to allow the land to rest from crop production every seventh year; after seven cycles of seven years, the fiftieth was to be a Jubilee year in which all debts were canceled, all slaves given their freedom, and vast land holdings redistributed. There is good reason to wonder if the Jews had ever actually observed this biblical commandment about forgiving debts and returning land to bankrupt families. Jesus announced from the very start of his ministry that the time had come to act on this requirement, which helps us understand why the wealthy and privileged were hostile to him from day one.

When he told his earliest disciples they would always have poor people among them, he was releasing neither them nor us from responsibility to the poor.[16] Jesus' teachings constantly highlighted the responsibility his followers had to care for the poorest and weakest members of society. The Parable of the Good Samaritan is probably the best-known story he ever told. Its story line has a man caring for someone of a different race and religion, and its conclusion is the challenge for everyone who hears it to "go and do likewise."[17]

The Parable of the Rich Fool takes on anyone who is so absorbed with taking care of himself that he forgets to look to eternity. An already-wealthy farmer who had a bumper crop thought only of himself and never of others. With not so much as a hint of sharing his bounty with someone whose crop might have failed that same year, the farmer could think only of building bigger storage buildings and having more for his retirement. His selfish insensitivity came up against this word from God: "You fool! This very night your life will be demanded from you. Then who will get what you have prepared for yourself?" And lest anyone should miss the point of the story, Jesus stated it explicitly: "This is how it will be with anyone who stores up things for himself but is not rich toward God."[18]

Although the Parable of the Unrighteous Steward has some particularly difficult features, the application of it is stated rather than implied. It is a parable about the financial dealing of Christ's disciples. "So if you have not been trustworthy in handling worldly wealth, who will trust you with true riches?" he asked. "No servant can serve two masters. Either he will hate the one and love the other, or he will be devoted to the one and despise the other. You cannot serve both God and Money."[19]

Living As Jesus Would Live

Wealth can lead to a spirit of arrogant self-sufficiency. Success may breed an inflated sense of one's personal importance. Living for the money and perks of this world will certainly kill sensitivity to the things of the Spirit. So what would Jesus do in our setting? What clues do we take from him as to how we should address the problem of poverty that exists around us? Following are four ways to imitate Jesus concerning the problem of poverty in our world.

REFLECT JESUS' ATTITUDE TOWARD THE POOR

We must learn to be in the world without being of the world, to use abundance without being held captive by it. His church must incarnate the message of love in meaningful actions. "If anyone has material possessions and sees his brother in need but has no pity on him, how can the love of God be in him? Dear children, let us not love with words or tongue but with actions and in truth."[20]

Don't hesitate to link arms with good works already in place that help people in need. Have a blood drive for the American Red Cross at your church. Link up with Habitat for Humanity, and perhaps several other churches in your area, to build a house for people in substandard living conditions. Lead a Bible study group at a local prison or help conduct Sunday worship at a nursing home. Work with a public school near you to provide school supplies for children from indigent families. You can think of dozens of ways to implement the love of God to people in need.

LEARN WHO YOUR NEIGHBORS ARE

If the Parable of the Good Samaritan teaches us anything, it demands that we cross racial, economic, and religious barriers to love and care for others. Do you really believe, for example, that people of other races are your neighbors? Assuming that your church is predominantly one race, how do you deal with people in your midst who are from other ethnic groups? Are your ministries indiscriminate as to race and ethnicity? There is no time in American culture when races are so segregated as on Sunday mornings! And the segregation by race in Sunday worship services frequently carries over into the ministries of those churches.

People with AIDS are your neighbors too. Since 1981, the world has been forced to come to terms with a deadly epidemic that is spread by sex, blood, and dirty drug needles. Because the disease is so devastating and because its spread is tied so directly to behaviors such as homosexuality and IV-drug use, Christians have reacted very poorly to its victims in many cases. Government agencies and service groups with their own agendas about sex and drugs have stepped in to supply what the followers of Jesus have been reluctant to do. Shame on us! The gospel is for all us sinners—stressed-out corporate executives, self-absorbed country-club women, and IV-drug abusers! Its message of repentance, forgiveness, and hope meets all of us at our deepest point of need.

LOVE MERCY MORE THAN PROSPERITY

The answer most of us give to the question *Why am I so fortunate as to have this?* appears to be the same one given by a little boy who found five dollars on the street: "So I can run to buy myself another toy."

I remember the big pitch of the college recruiter who came to Middleton High School in the spring of 1963. He rattled off statistics about expected lifetime earnings to show that people who get a college education could expect to make many times more money over a lifetime than their peers without a college education. Fortunately I had an English teacher who had taken an interest in me and had already spoken to me about college. But I don't ever remember Mrs. Oldham saying anything about money. She spoke instead of doing something worthwhile with my life, finding a way to make the world a little better place to live, and doing something to help others.

I don't often think of the late Mrs. Oldham, I confess. But she came to mind when I read this from Richard J. Foster:

> Do we see a college education, for example, as a ticket to privilege or as a training for service to the needy? What do we teach our teenagers in this matter? Do we urge them to enter college because it will better equip them to serve? Or do we try to bribe them with promises of future status and salary increases? No wonder they graduate more deeply concerned about their standard of living than about suffering humanity.[21]

Maybe it isn't too late for all of us to think again about why we have certain things.

- Why do you have your natural gifts and talents?
- Why do you have the job you have?
- Why do you have your education?
- Why do you have money?
- Why do you have an apartment or house?
- Why do you have a car?
- Why do you have access to a particular resource?

If the answers to these questions come back in the first person only, you need to rethink the early programming someone gave you and reconsider your present life priorities. In addition to what these things mean for your personal benefit, they are supposed to fit into a divine plan for loving God and your neighbor.

TAKE UP THE CAUSE OF THE POOR

If we truly desire to recapture the life and spirit of the first-century church, here are a couple of texts to consider: "Selling their possessions and goods, they gave to anyone as he had need."[22] And, "No one claimed that any of his possessions was his own, but they shared everything they had."[23] Yet there is nothing to indicate that this sharing dehumanized people or made them dependent on charity.

Christian distinctiveness in today's culture must include an alternative attitude toward the consumer-oriented focus of many people. We can simplify our lives in various ways in order to do more for others. That may mean a more modest house, less-expensive transportation, or even a change in vocation. The Spirit of God will guide these decisions for believers who have allowed themselves to be sensitized to human need.

How Much Do We Need?

Leo Tolstoy's *How Much Land Does a Man Need?* raises a critical issue. The main character in the story was told he could have all the land he could encircle on foot in one day. The man started off with the intention to claim only what he could care for and use productively. As time passed, however, he began to desire more and more. As the day was about to end, it became apparent that it would be almost impossible to get back to his point of beginning. Struggling to do so, he fell dead from a heart attack. The only land he received was the tiny plot in which he was buried.

This prayer by Peter Marshall is one that all of us tempted by materialism should pray regularly.

> Forbid it, Lord, that our roots become too firmly attached to this earth, that we should fall in love with things.
>
> Help us to understand that the pilgrimage of this life is but an introduction, a preface, a training school for what is to come.
>
> Then shall we see all of life in its true perspective. Then shall we not fall in love with the things of time, but come to love the things that endure. Then shall we be saved from the tyranny of possessions which we have no leisure to enjoy, of property whose care becomes a burden. Give us, we pray, the courage to simplify our lives. Amen.[24]

Money is not evil or dirty. It is only the "love of money" that is rebuked in the Bible.[25] Therefore the term "wealthy Christian" need not be an oxymoron. I know several very wealthy people who use their wealth and power to honor the Lord Jesus Christ, rather than to aggrandize themselves. They model the spirit of Christ that Paul wrote about:

> Command those who are rich in this present world not to be arrogant nor to put their hope in wealth, which is so

uncertain, but to put their hope in God, who richly provides us with everything for our enjoyment. Command
them to do good, to be rich in good deeds, and to be generous and willing to share. In this way they will lay up
treasure for themselves as a firm foundation for the coming age, so that they may take hold of the life that is truly
life.[26]

What do you think Jesus would have done with the money
Imelda Marcos spent on shoes in her poverty-stricken country?
What do you think he would do with the fortune of the wealthiest
person you know? What would Jesus do with what you have?

*Being poor in and of itself is neither virtuous or ignominious. Rather,
how we use our wealth indicates whether our heart's desire is to serve self
or to follow Jesus.*

Lord, thou hast said that our Father in heaven notes even the fall of a sparrow to the ground. Help us to believe, O God, that thou art concerned not only with the rolling of the spheres in their orbits, but even with each of us, our doubts, and perplexities.

We remember all too well the bitter discoveries we have made when we have tried to run our lives our own way, when we try to steer our own craft.

Wilt thou come aboard, Lord Jesus, and set us a true course, for we grow weary of life's demands, tired of our own blundering ways.

We seek a clear light to shine upon our troubled way.

We ask thee to give us clearer directions.

Where we have missed the way and wandered far, bring us back at whatever cost to our pride.

Take away our stubborn self-will, for we know that in thy will alone is our peace.

We seek that peace.

Catherine Marshall, Editor, *The Prayers of Peter Marshall*

CHAPTER TEN

Confusion

Humans are notorious for desiring simple answers to complex problems. Is life a simple exercise in good and evil choices? Are all issues black and white?

The question here is not *Do good and evil exist?* but *Are all choices clearly between good and evil options?* Put another way, the issue is not finding a way to defend moral objectivity against moral relativism but learning how to deal with moral obscurity. Perhaps a few illustrations will clarify what is at stake in this chapter.

There are political challenges on which faithful Christians take contradictory stances. Their polar-opposite conclusions have nothing to do with a lack of spiritual sensitivity on the part of anyone but on the complexity of circumstances involved.

For example, as the world's single remaining superpower, the United States is the world's peacekeeper. Should we put soldiers in harm's way in Korea, the Middle East, or Eastern Europe? Should we undertake humanitarian relief efforts with American troops in Africa, and then run the risk of getting caught between warring tribal factions while trying to deliver food and medicine? Everyone seems to "lean" to one side or the other on this issue.

Abortion is an even more more complex social problem than some of us have acknowledged. That failure of acknowledgment is a key to our failure to solve this problem. A principled stand by believers requires a strong antiabortion posture, but are there no complex cases that leave your opposition less than unqualified? There are rare-but-actual cases where the choice is between the life of the mother and the life of the early-stage baby she is carrying. There is also the issue of someone who is pregnant because of rape rather than consent. I have been in situations where these decisions had to be made—and there have been conflicting conclusions reached by equally devout persons.

Again, what about the situation reported in February of 1996 concerning a twenty-nine-year-old woman who had been comatose since an automobile accident ten years earlier. Someone raped her in her nursing home, and she was four and one-half months along when she was discovered to be pregnant. Her Catholic parents rejected the alternative of abortion. Was this their moral obligation? Was it their choice? Might other parents or guardians have made a different decision on her behalf without doing something morally wrong? Only a fanatic is always and without qualification either for or against abortion, regardless of the circumstances. The issue is far too complex for such simplicity.

Personal problems are the most confusing of all. Currently, I am trying to help a woman work through a difficult situation: Her husband has abused her for years. He has demeaned her in private, humiliated her in public, and beaten her badly enough to send her to the hospital twice. She is from a church and parental background that keeps telling her that she has no right to leave her scoundrel husband because he hasn't committed adultery. Hold on! Before you are so cocksure that you know what she should do, let me remind you that you are not in her shoes. If you tell her to run from her husband's abuse, how will you help her deal with what her parents and church will do with her? Both have threatened her with still more abuse if she leaves. Her church will revoke her membership and her parents will not allow her to come into their house. Perhaps it is simple to you and me only because we are not in her shoes. She is confused to the point of being on the brink of either a complete emotional collapse or suicide.

Suppose your neighbor calls you about his seventeen-year-old son who has just been picked up on a DUI charge. This isn't the boy's first alcohol-related problem, and both you and your neighbor know something is going to have to get his attention about the seriousness of his problem. So your friend asks, "Should I let him stay in the drunk tank overnight? Should I stop pampering him and covering up for him and let him suffer the consequences of drinking?" Be careful how you answer even this theoretical question. It is absolutely necessary for the boy to be hauled up short for what he is doing. Maybe a night in jail is the way to make that happen. But what if he gets beaten up? What if he is raped? How do you live with your advice to that neighbor then? It's far more complex a problem, and requires a lot of thought before this multifaceted question is answered. You'd better help your neighbor think through his decision and remind him that you can't and won't take the responsibility of making the decision for him.

In this series of studies on developing the mind of Christ, how shall we view these convoluted and painful choices? "If we had Jesus' insight and relationship with the Father," says someone, "we could be spared these personal confusions. Everything would be clear for us." Are you sure?

How Jesus Lived

Even Jesus had occasional sleepless nights, and the Gospels document his anguish over sheep without shepherds and hard choices he was called on to make. "One of those days Jesus went out to a mountainside to pray, and spent the night praying to God. When morning came, he called his disciples to him and chose twelve of them, whom he also designated apostles."[1] And after that sleepless night of agonizing prayer, he still chose Judas to be in the group!

The most intense and anguished night of Christ's life was the one before his crucifixion. The word Gethsemane means "oil press," and this place turned out to be a place where Jesus' humanity was in full view. He dealt with a range of feelings that night—fear, confusion, doubt, frustration, and anger. It was a night not fundamentally different from ones that someone reading this page might recall.

> On reaching the place, he said to them, "Pray that you will not fall into temptation." He withdrew about a stone's throw beyond them, knelt down and prayed, "Father, if you are willing, take this cup from me; yet not my will, but yours be done." An angel from heaven appeared to him and strengthened him. And being in anguish, he prayed more earnestly, and his sweat was like drops of blood falling to the ground.[2]

Can you visualize such a scene? Jesus was "in anguish" that night. His prayers became so intense and his soul was so burdened, that sweat rolled off his body as if he were already wounded and bleeding. Either that was a melodramatic imitation of personal confusion or a real night of heart-rending perplexity. Because I believe Jesus was authentic rather than phony, I can only see it as the latter.

The Gethsemane experience of Jesus parallels the ordeals his followers have faced across the centuries of Christian history.

When we are in situations with multiple options and uncertain outcomes, Christ knows our feelings. He understands the wrestlings that are going on in our minds and souls. He has lived them in human history.

Life is not the simple either/or, black/white, right/wrong event some pretend it to be. God sometimes denies us the comfort of certitude when we are forced to make difficult decisions about problems that have unforeseeable outcomes. This is the way real life works, and this is the world of personal confusion in which all of us participate.

WHAT JESUS TAUGHT

Having the mind of Christ often involves clear and unambiguous certainty. For example, the dictum that guided his life is stated in his own words: "My food is to do the will of him who sent me and to finish his work."[3] In such a statement, he was reflecting a straightforward teaching of Scripture. For example, the same thing is said in these words: "Now all has been heard; here is the conclusion of the matter: Fear God and keep his commandments, for this is the whole duty of man. For God will bring every deed into judgment, including every hidden thing, whether it is good or evil."[4]

My opinion is that we sometimes pretend life is more complex than it is in order to avoid sacrifice, self-denial, or suffering. For every issue as thorny and complex as the ones mentioned in the opening paragraphs of this chapter, there are thousands that are altogether unambiguous. Foreign aid is a tough subject, but my obligation to help a family where sickness has created poverty for them is manifest and obvious. "Anyone who does not love his brother, whom he has seen, cannot love God, whom he has not seen."[5] My selfishness may cause me to withhold help, but there is no doubt what I *should* do in that situation. Yes, some abortion decisions are exceedingly complex, call for more prayer than dogmatism, and require some degree of tolerance for different perspectives. But our nation's abortion-on-demand culture that glibly uses a medical solution for either immorality (i.e., fornication) or irresponsibility (i.e., a married couple's failure to use appropriate birth control) is simply wrong.

When right and wrong are clearly defined in Scripture, the only remaining question is our faithfulness to God. The Bible says that such things as lying, stealing, profane uses of God's name, drunkenness, and the like are sinful. These issues are not open for debate regarding their appropriateness or inappropriateness to the lifestyle of a Christian. They are out of place in every place for God's people. Choosing to make one of these things part of my behavior could not be due to confusion, but would be willful sin against God.

Even so, Jesus himself encountered and spoke to some situations of ambiguity in his ministry. Take the incident involving a woman "caught in the act of adultery."[6] Where is the ambiguity there? There is none with regard to the law against adultery and the penalty for committing so serious a sin. Neither, apparently, was there any ambiguity in the fact that the woman was in fact "caught" and guilty as charged. But there were some questions as to what should be done with her.

Under the Law of Moses, a clear distinction was made between acts of fornication and adultery. Both were serious violations of the law of God, but one was considerably more serious than the other. Fornication was a sexual act involving two unmarried persons, and the penalty for it is specified in Exodus 22:16–17. The couple either had to marry or, if the girl's father refused to let her marry the man involved, he had to pay a sum of money that would presumably become part of her dowry. Adultery, on the other hand, was regarded as a far more serious sin. Its gravity appears to be in the fact that adultery is not even necessarily a sexual act. Its essence is trust breaking or the violation of a solemn covenant. For a man or woman to have sexual intercourse with a person other than his wife or her husband was clearly a violation of the holy marriage covenant between them. Proving oneself "faithless" to a marriage covenant could bring down a death sentence under certain circumstances.[7]

The woman of John 8 was neither a prostitute nor an unmarried woman who had been seduced. She was either a married woman or knowingly involved with a married man; she was not merely having sex with someone to whom she was not married, but she was consciously repudiating the holy covenant of marriage. There was no defense to be made of her, and even though her accusers were wrong in their motives (i.e., attempting to trap Jesus), they were apparently correct in saying that her action was serious enough to deserve death.

Jesus' real dilemma in this case was not the one his accusers thought they had created for him—either loyalty to the Law of Moses or high-handed disregard of its statutes. His dilemma was how to balance his concern to obey the Law in all its particulars versus his desire to bring the offending woman to repentance and salvation. An easy form of black-and-white thinking would have allowed him to say, "Yes, she does deserve to die. Since you brought her behavior to light, though, I refuse to be involved in stoning her. See to the matter yourselves." But Jesus didn't take the easy way out; he sought a way to bring hope and the opportunity for salvation to the woman.

Jesus appears to have played the game of "legalistic righteousness" with the men who had brought this case before him—and to have gone them one better. It seems that he appealed to a "technicality" in the Law of Moses that prohibits anyone with advance knowledge of a violation of the moral-criminal code from giving evidence against a transgressor.[8] He at times used a similar method of argument about Sabbath observance.[9]

What was Jesus' point in these situations? It certainly was not to nullify, set aside, or discount the Law of Moses. Neither was it to minimize the seriousness of human sin. His point was, instead, to affirm human dignity in the face of assaults on it and to make the point that divine law was always to be interpreted and applied in favor of pardon and healing rather than stringent judgment.

"The Sabbath was made for man, not man for the Sabbath"[10] is a particular application of a much broader truth. God's laws free, ennoble, and empower persons; they are not to be seen as the means to manipulate and destroy them. For first-century Pharisees or us, it is a good thing to ask whether our interpretation of a text or biblical law is blessing or bludgeoning people. If it is principally doing the latter, the interpretation needs to be reexamined.

We sometimes find ourselves in similar situations, but without the wisdom of Jesus. We want to do the right thing "by the letter of the law" but also want to hold out the prospect of redemption. Lest someone reply to this alleged dilemma by saying again that these two goals can never be in conflict, perhaps it will help to look at an Old Testament case study in personal confusion.

A CASE STUDY IN COMPLEXITY

Abraham followed the custom of his place and time when he had a child-heir by Hagar. With both him and his wife well advanced in years, he listened to Sarah's counsel about attempting to have a son by her handmaid. According to well-documented custom in the Ancient Near East, Sarah said, "Go, sleep with my maidservant; perhaps I can build a family through her."[11]

When Hagar became pregnant and gave birth to a son, things quickly became muddled and ugly. "When she knew she was pregnant, she began to despise [Sarah]."[12] Sarah, in turn, resented Hagar's condescending spirit and appealed to her husband to set things right. Trying to wash his hands of the unfolding problems, he told Sarah to do whatever she wished with her pregnant maidservant. Sarah so abused and mistreated Hagar that she took her son, Ishmael, and ran away from Abraham's family and compound.[13]

Before someone replies to this scene of misery with the explanation that things were out of control because Abraham and Sarah ran ahead of God and did not wait for him to fulfill his promise about a son, let me concede the point. They were wrong on a variety of points. But it is not their perplexity that is at issue. What about poor Hagar?

Imagine the confusion thrust upon Hagar by all that had happened. The suggestion of "surrogate motherhood" was not hers. Once that choice was made by her master and mistress, she had no choice in the matter; slaves in the ancient world were not consulted about their wishes! So, what is to become of a woman who has fled from her home to avoid further abuse and who has a small child with her? (Other women still face this issue in their lives.)

An angel appeared to Hagar near a desert spring on the road to Shur and asked what she was doing there. "I'm running away from my mistress," she said.[14] Here was the angel's counsel: "Go back to your mistress and submit to her."[15] And so the groundwork was laid for the bitter relationship between Ishmael and Isaac and their descendants across four millennia.

Even with a word from God through an angel, this story did not have a happy ending. Sound familiar? Some life situations become so confusing that even with repentance, forgiveness, and transformed personalities things never work out to heal broken relationships and make life work as it should.

Hagar went away from her experience with the angel at the spring with only one assurance: God saw and cared about what was happening with her. "She gave this name to the Lord who spoke to her: 'You are the God who sees me,' for she said, 'I have now seen the One who sees me.' That is why the well was called Beer Lahai Roi [Hebrew: Well of the Living One Who Sees Me]."[16] That God cares about what happens in our personal distresses is no small comfort, but he does not snap his fingers and produce fairy-tale endings to them.

WHAT CREATES OUR CONFUSION?

What things are most likely going to be responsible for our human agonies and problems? Three things seem to be constant to them.

1. SUFFERING

Suffering, or the prospect of suffering, can throw our lives into confusion. It was the prospect of being separated from the Father and Holy Spirit on the cross that had Jesus in anguish in Gethsemane. Paul wrestled with the presence of chronic illness and suffering in his life.[17] And Job was tormented by Satan in an effort to undermine and destroy his faith.

Human beings still face the same confusion in sickness, unemployment, the death of a child, a parent's extended suffering, etc. The heartaches accompanying such things are very real, and only one who has never felt any of them could dismiss their seriousness. Sometimes one's only certainty in these situations is Hagar's knowledge that God sees and cares.

2. INJUSTICE

We are justifiably confused, angry, and frightened when we realize the wrong side seems to be winning. People literally get away with murder these days. Meanwhile, honest workers get fired, good people are lied about, and innocent people go to jail. But ours is not the first generation in which injustice seemed to have the upper hand.

Remember the story of a seventeen-year-old boy whose brothers sold him as a slave to some traders headed toward Egypt? Both the story and a young man's personal agony over why something like this was happening to him are real. And there were lies, prison, and broken promises along his path. For thirteen long years, he was a perpetual victim of evil. Only when he was elevated to be the Vizier of Egypt at age thirty did anything good appear as a possible outcome to his ordeal.[18]

3. UNRESOLVED PROBLEMS

Sometimes, we simply don't see how things can work out for us. Believers know that our God has made this wonderful promise to us: "And we know that in all things God works for the good of those who love him, who have been called according to his purpose."[19] But we want to know when and how he will keep that promise! At the very least, we want to experience the resolution ourselves—but that doesn't always happen either. Just think of all the people who died and were buried in Egypt between the times of Joseph and Moses. They knew their captivity was cruel and abusive. They also knew that God had made promises to Abraham and his descendants. But where was he?

There is an interesting contrast in the final part of Hebrews 11. Beginning at verse 32, the writer gives a long list of heroes—Gideon, Samson, David, and others—who conquered, triumphed, and received victory as the outcome of their faith. In the middle of verse 35, and in the next four verses, however, the praise is for those faithful people of God who were tortured without release, denied home and family, imprisoned, and killed. There is no guarantee that you will see the resolution of your problem or the vindication of your cause in your lifetime on earth. Your reward—like those people in Hebrews 11:35—may come only in the life that is to follow. You may have to finish your course on Planet Earth in chronic illness, suffering as a victim of injustice, or without a family of your own. If so, your prayers may be similar to this one by Henri Nouwen:

> I call to you, O Lord, from my quiet darkness. Show me your mercy and love. Let me see your face, hear your voice, touch the hem of your cloak. I want to love you, be with you, speak to you and simply stand in your presence.
>
> But I cannot make it happen. Pressing my eyes against my hands is not praying, and reading about your presence is not living in it.
>
> But there is that moment in which you will come to me, as you did to your fearful disciples, and say, "Do not be afraid; it is I."

Let that moment come soon, O Lord. And if you want to delay it, then make me patient. Amen.[20]

PULLING YOURSELF TO THE ROCK

If you have not been there already, you will someday be in the position our Savior was in Gethsemane. When he told the disciples "The spirit is willing, but the body is weak,"[21] he was not talking about them but himself. He was in authentic agony on that terrible night! He was ready to do the will of his Father, for that was the nourishment that sustained him. Yet he was wrestling with the limitations of his human frailty. Harry Emerson Fosdick helps us reflect on Jesus' struggle in Gethsemane:

> Consider the battlefield of Gethsemane. Was there ever a more eventful engagement than that? It was a struggle for clear vision to see and strength to do the will of God. Peter Annet, an old Deist, used to say that praying men are like sailors who have cast anchor on a rock, and who imagine they are pulling the rock to themselves, when they are really pulling themselves to the rock. But that is a caricature of what praying men at their best think. The master here was deliberately trying to pull himself to the rock. That was the objective of the struggle in the garden.
>
> The will of God was settled; [Jesus] wanted clearly to see it and strongly to be apprehended by it, and he called God in to fight the narrower self will that opposed the larger devotion. What a deep experience such praying brings into any life that knows it![22]

When you do find yourself in Jesus' situation, you can do no better than he did that night. In doing as he did, you will have his mind through your ordeal. He took his concerns to the Father in prayer. He was totally and transparently honest about his fears. And he submitted to the unfolding circumstances that lay ahead for him in the confidence that he would be given the strength to endure.

Heaven sent an angel to minister to Jesus that night,[23] and who is to say that he would do any less for you?

If I were asked for a yardstick to discern good from bad spirituality, I would suggest three criteria to be detached from: material gain, self-importance and the urge to dominate others. Unfortunately, much of what is labeled spirituality in America today moves in the opposite direction. It means using the names of God and Christ to promote one's own importance, material gain and right to oppress others.

Rosemary Radford Ruether, quoted in *Toxic Faith*

CHAPTER ELEVEN

Religion

I've only been in the Holy Land once, although I want to go back someday for a more extended tour. I spent my time in and around Jerusalem, trying to retrace the events of the last week of the life of my Lord. It was a deeply moving experience. To visit Gethsemane, to stand in Pilate's Judgment Hall, to walk along the Via Dolorosa; each experience affirmed the link in my mind between history and faith, fact and theology.

There were negative parts to the trip that made it problematic at times. It wasn't so much that there were crowds of people and hucksters selling their wares. After all, Jerusalem was a bustling city when Jesus was there. The city was packed with extra tens of thousands of Passover pilgrims when Jesus played out the final drama of his ministry.

The problem for me was at the critical sites themselves. Almost every one has been claimed and built upon by churches. And the construction is invariably of such a nature that it obscures what you are trying to see. Shared locations are the worst of all, for in attempting to carve up the area so everyone can enshrine part of it, chaos obscures any sense of Christ's lingering presence that might otherwise have been sensed.

As I reflected on what I had experienced, I thought how similar it had been to what humanity has experienced across the centuries. Churches often get in the way of people's attempts to see Jesus! Our division, hypocrisy, and other sins obscure rather than preserve Christ's lingering presence in the world. Religion gets in God's way!

RELIGION AND IRRELIGION

In case you haven't noticed it, the Bible is littered with "strange" stories of heroism among people who were out of step with the religious norms of their time.

Once, a king had to take leadership in leading the Israelites to observe their holy independence day, Passover. After the collapse of the Northern Kingdom in 721 B.C. and in connection with the cleansing of the Jerusalem Temple, King Hezekiah took the initiative. He sent messengers not only to the people of Judah, but throughout Israel as well to invite people to keep the Passover at Jerusalem. Although some were "out of the habit" and turned a deaf ear to the invitation, thousands of others began moving toward the city.

The Passover lamb was killed and the celebration began. Some from the north arrived too late to perform the purifications that required several days. So, although they "had not purified themselves, yet they ate the Passover, contrary to what was written."[1] Religionists must have been going crazy about their impurity and unauthorized feasting. "But Hezekiah prayed for them, saying, 'May the Lord, who is good, pardon everyone who sets his heart on seeking God—the Lord, the God of his fathers— even if he is not clean according to the rules of the sanctuary.' And the Lord heard Hezekiah and healed the people."[2]

What a magnanimous attitude and prayer on the king's part. And what a gracious response from the Lord to forgive the people. God is not so bound by his laws that he cannot exhibit mercy. This is a lesson that religionists seem never to see in Scripture or practice in their own lives. How many church fights and divisions have resulted from disagreement over issues less clear-cut than this one? How many have been settled and healed with such gentleness? And notice that it was the king rather than the priests who took the lead in this issue. Many people have been run off by churches because they saw religious warring run roughshod over spiritual leadership.

Amos prophesied about seven hundred years before the birth of Jesus and decried the religion of his generation. Speaking for Yahweh, he declared:

> I hate, I despise your religious feasts; I cannot stand your assemblies. Even though you bring me burnt offerings and grain offerings, I will not accept them. Though you bring choice fellowship offerings, I will have no regard for them. Away with the noise of your songs! I will not listen to the music of your harps.[3]

Hadn't the Lord commanded those assemblies, offerings, and songs? Indeed, he had. But the religionmongers had made them ends in themselves. They had forgotten that worship and gifts were means to the end of transforming the lives of people. "But let justice roll on like a river, righteousness like a never-failing stream," the Lord commanded.[4] Religious rituals separated from heart-involvement and life-transformation are evil, for they supply the people who "play church" with them a false sense of security.

Isaiah hammered home the same theme. "New Moons, Sab-baths and convocations—I cannot bear your evil assemblies. Your New Moon festivals and your appointed feasts my soul hates. They have become a burden to me; I am weary of bearing them," said Yahweh to the people. "Stop doing wrong, learn to do right! Seek justice, encourage the oppressed. Defend the cause of the fatherless, plead the case of the widow."[5]

The twelve-step program that originated with Alcoholics Anonymous has made a very insightful distinction in its vocabu-lary between religion and spirituality. *Religion* refers to the institu-tions, rituals, and authority figures of churches; many people battling addictions have been hurt by these. *Spirituality*, on the other hand, is one's sincere and genuine openness to the work of a Higher Power in his or her life. Some churches would do well to teach and practice this distinction.

Permit me to be more precise still about the difference I see between religion (i.e. authentic Christian faith)[6] and religionism. I do not want to be heard by anyone as being irreverent, refusing the legitimate authority of God, or rebelling against the holy. Follow-ing the distinction made in the preceding paragraph, I am using the term "religionism" in this chapter to refer to the human effort to control people in the name of God, truth, and righteousness. Yes, it is the Jim Jones's and David Koresh's use of the Bible that I have in mind. But it is also the more common manipulation of human minds and freedoms that we have all witnessed in main-stream churches and other religious enterprises.

Although it presents an eclectic, if not New Age, interpreta-tion of Jesus, a book from a few years back draws out the theme I am trying to clarify. The central figure has the following conversa-tion with a questioner:

> "You seem to be an intelligent fellow, Josh," Herm said, moving to a serious vein, "what do you think of reli-gion?"
>
> "What do you mean by religion? Do you mean the

way it is or the way God intended it to be? There's a big difference, you know."

"Well, the way it is, the way the churches run it."

"God never intended that religion become what it is today. Jesus came to earth to try to free people from that kind of regimented religion where people are threatened if they don't obey rules and rituals invented by the clergy. Jesus came to teach people that they are God's children and, as God's children, they are free, free to grow as human beings, to become beautiful people as God intended. That can't be legislated. Jesus gave the apostles and the community as a support to provide help and guidance and consolation. Jesus did not envision bosses in the worldly sense. He wanted his apostles to guide and serve, not to dictate and legislate like those who govern this world. Unfortunately, religious leaders model themselves after civil governments and treat people accordingly. In this they fall into the same trap that the scribes and Pharisees fell into, making religion a tangible set of measurable religious observances, which is legalistic and superficial. In doing this they become the focus of religious observance rather than God, and it is their endless rules and their rituals rather than the love of God and concern for others that occupy the people's attention.

"Customs and practices and traditions then replace true service of God, and these become a serious obstacle to real growth in the love of God. If people take religious leaders too seriously, they become rigid in their thinking and afraid to think for themselves, and must always refer decisions to the clergy. Even as adults they will still cling to the religious practices of their childhood, and when even ceremonies and mere customs change they panic, because they have been led to believe these things were their faith. . . ."

Finally Herm broke the silence, saying to Joshua, "You really feel strongly about this, don't you?"

"Yes," Joshua answered, "because Jesus never intended that religion do the damage to people that it has. . . . The function of religious leaders is to set an example, to draw people to God by their own deep faith and by the purity of their personal lives, not intimidate people into sterile external observance. That is not religion. That mocks true religion.

"True religion comes from the heart. It is a deep relationship with God, and should bring peace and joy and love to people, not fear and guilt and meanness."[7]

The experience and teachings of Jesus as recorded in the Gospels confirm the claim that he encountered the painful distinction between spirituality and religionism. How he reacted to the use of religion to bully and hurt people becomes the standard by which we may measure our feelings and actions today. What would Jesus do about a religion that gets in the way of people trying to experience God in their lives? We are not left to wonder how this question might be answered.

How Jesus Lived

One of the most regulation-encumbered elements of life in Jesus' immediate environment was the Sabbath. The Sabbath was not only a distinctive feature of Jewish religion, but an oppressive one. What had been intended to be a delightful experience for individuals and families had become a heavy-handed, hateful event.

The Law of Moses required that the Sabbath be kept as a time of rest, devotion to God, and relationship building among friends and family. But the rabbis took the prohibition against work on that holy day and began tracing out its "implications"—according to their best understanding. A long tractate of the Mishnah lists thirty-nine forbidden actions that could not be performed on Saturday. Among them are such things as moving an object from one place to another, separating two threads, writing as many as two letters from the alphabet, tying a knot, etc. Each of these prohibitions generated debate in turn as to what constituted an offense within the category. Did an artificial limb, for example, constitute an offense of carrying a burden? Some rabbis said it did, but others disagreed!

Jesus continually ran afoul of Sabbath regulations that had evolved within Judaism. For example, on a particular Saturday he was teaching in a synagogue and saw a woman "who had been crippled by a spirit for eighteen years." He was moved with compassion for her plight and said, "Woman, you are set free from your infirmity." When he touched her, she was healed immediately. "Indignant because Jesus had healed on the Sabbath, the synagogue ruler said to the people, 'There are six days for work. So come and be healed on those days, not on the Sabbath.' "[8]

Can you believe it! A woman crippled for nearly two decades was well, and the preacher could not celebrate her good fortune. He saw healing on the Sabbath as a violation of the Law of Moses and was critical of what had taken place. "The Lord answered him, 'You hypocrites! Doesn't each of you on the Sabbath untie his ox or donkey from the stall and lead it out to give it water? Then should not this woman, a daughter of Abraham, whom Satan has kept bound for eighteen long years, be set free on the Sabbath day from what bound her?' "[9]

Jesus also got into trouble because he ignored some "purity laws" his elders had created and bound. They had decided, for example, that one could not eat food with "unclean" hands. The uncleanness here was purely ceremonial and had nothing to do with hygiene. "The Pharisees and all the Jews do not eat unless they give their hands a ceremonial washing, holding to the tradition of the elders," explains Mark. "When they come from the marketplace they do not eat unless they wash. And they observe many other traditions, such as the washing of cups, pitchers and kettles."[10]

When some of Jesus' disciples were observed eating without going through the hand-washing ritual, the religionists criticized the Lord for not teaching them this "important rule." Jesus would not concede the point and did not require his disciples to embrace their rule. The issue, after all, was not washing but control. Jesus represented a threat to the establishment of his day because he would not march to the cadence they were calling. He would have no part of such gamesmanship and hypocrisy. "He replied, 'Isaiah was right when he prophesied about you hypocrites; as it is written: These people honor me with their lips, but their hearts are far from me. They, worship me in vain; their teachings are but rules taught by men.' "[11]

WHAT JESUS TAUGHT

Jesus went head-on with formalistic, legalistic religion in Matthew 23. As translated by Eugene Peterson in *The Message*, the force of his encounter with the "religion scholars and Pharisees" comes through powerfully. In reading it, one should remember that Christianity as well as Judaism has generated this same phenomenon. And what did Jesus say about it?

RELIGIONISM KEEPS PEOPLE FROM GOD

Religionism keeps people from the kingdom of God. "I've had it with you! You're hopeless, you religion scholars, you Pharisees! Frauds! Your lives are roadblocks to God's kingdom. You refuse to enter, and won't let anyone else in either."[12] True religion teaches a believer to "be a servant" to others.[13] Phony religion insists on special garb and deference to leaders, titles, and perks for them. Can we not see how out of character such things would be for Jesus? Can we not see how they turn people off to Christianity? Authentic Christian leaders imitate Jesus' example of serving others and do not demand to be served.

RELIGIONISM BREEDS EXTREMES

Remember what the Jews did with Saturday? Christians once did the same things with Sunday. No playing with the kids. No lawn cutting at the widow's house down the street. Just dark clothes, somber faces, and scowls all around! "You're hopeless, you religion scholars and Pharisees! Frauds! You go halfway around the world to make a convert, but once you get him you make him into a replica of yourselves, double-damned."[14]

RELIGIONISM GENERATES HAIRSPLITTING

Bad religion makes ridiculous distinctions that miss the point of holy living.

> You're hopeless! What arrogant stupidity! You say, "If someone makes a promise with his fingers crossed, that's nothing; but if he swears with his hand on the Bible, that's serious." What ignorance! Does the leather on the Bible carry more weight than the skin on your hands? And what about this piece of trivia: "If you shake hands on a promise, that's nothing; but if you raise your hand that God is your witness, that's serious"? What ridiculous hairsplitting! What difference does it make whether you shake hands or raise hands? A promise is a promise. What difference does it make if you make your promise inside or outside a house of worship? A promise is a promise. God is present, watching and holding you to account regardless.[15]

In a masterful article titled "Is the Church Interested in the Kingdom?" Christian Smith explores this tendency toward nit-picking legalism. Conservative, evangelical churches have displayed a fondness for enjoining abstinence from relatively trivial things ranging from dancing, to card playing, to movies. Boys and girls are banned from going swimming together. Boys can wear shorts, but girls can't. Nobody who smokes can lead a public prayer, etc. Here is Smith's analysis of why we do this:

> The reason is because, when it comes to the relatively important things in life (basic values and behavior concerning wealth, power, prestige, justice, security, peace, work, time, and so on), most Christians are indistinguishable from the world. Still, Christians know that they should be different from the world in some way—otherwise, what would Christianity mean at all? So, in an effort to establish some kind of Christian distinctiveness, attention and concern is focused on the trivial (which, by its very nature, does not require us to make difficult changes in our lives).[16]

That's how phony faith works. In fact, that's exactly what Jesus states in Matthew 23.

RELIGIONISM REPLACES SPIRITUALITY WITH RITUAL

> You're hopeless, you religion scholars and Pharisees! Frauds! You keep meticulous account books, tithing on every nickel and dime you get, but on the meat of God's Law, things like fairness and compassion and commitment—the absolute basics!—you carelessly take it or leave it. Careful bookkeeping is commendable, but the basics are required. Do you have any idea how silly you look, writing a life story that's wrong from start to finish, nitpicking over commas and semicolons?[17]

RELIGIONISM FOCUSES ON EXTERNALS

> You're hopeless, you religion scholars and Pharisees! Frauds! You're like manicured grave plots, grass clipped and the flowers bright, but six feet down it's all rotting bones and worm-eaten flesh. People look at you and

think you're saints, but beneath the skin you're total frauds.[18]

Jesus was incredibly severe with the sort of thing we're all guilty of at times. Religionism allows external behavior to supplant internal Christlikeness. Church attendance makes up for one person's selfishness. Teetotaling gets another person off for being a racist. Carrying a Bible under his arm on Sunday morning evens the score for the pornographic movie he rented Thursday. This sort of phoniness in the name of Christianity must stop!

WHAT JESUS OFFERS

Most of us have become familiar with the widely accepted manner of referring to life's most destructive behaviors as *addictive behaviors*. Drunkenness, habitual lying, compulsive gambling, unrestrained spending: These and other actions are termed *addictive*. Contrary to the early fears of some, the use of this term in our culture is not an attempt to help people avoid taking responsibility for their lives. Instead, this term identifies a harmful component of one's lifestyle and challenges him or her to take positive steps to get free of its control. The best known of these approaches is the highly successful twelve-step method of Alcoholics Anonymous previously mentioned.

Scripture certainly supports this view of human behavior. Jesus spoke of sin's power to addict or enslave,[19] and Paul wrote of a mind-set that is not only hostile to God's will but incapable of obeying it.[20] Do you know what one of the latest identified addictions is? Religion! But this recent "discovery" was documented long ago in Scripture. Practically any good thing—whether money, sex, medicine, or religion—can be addictive and enslaving when used in ways God never intended.

Religion addicts don't believe in God so much as they believe in some system that is supposed to deliver or manipulate him. The Pharisees in general and preconversion Paul in particular make good candidates for religion addicts. They believed and

taught that God was at the end of a series of legalistic require-
ments.[21] They believed they could wring a blessing out of God by
following the detailed traditions they had built around Scripture.
Paul's solution to his enslavement to religionism was not atheism,
but Jesus. "I consider everything a loss compared to the surpass-
ing greatness of knowing Christ Jesus my Lord, for whose sake I
have lost all things."[22]

Working the angles of a religious system produces frustration,
intolerance, hypocrisy, and failure. The void in the human soul
that can only be filled by God goes begging. Only a personal relationship with God through Christ can satisfy the need for love,
acceptance, and security that all people feel instinctively. Seen in
the way it often works, religion as a human effort to control people
in the name of God, truth, and righteousness came to an end with
Jesus. Jesus' alternative to religionism may be summarized in five
concepts:

1. RELATIONSHIP-ORIENTED FAITH

Authentic faith is always relationship-oriented rather than
system-oriented. As opposed to offering a "plan" or "system," the
Bible teaches that all spiritual issues ultimately reduce to two great
commandments about loving God and one's neighbor. It is love for
God that keeps a believer free of the world's seductions and pol-
lutions. It is love for neighbor that makes him or her sensitive to
people in distress. Addictive approaches to religion pile up good
works and try to win acceptance. True religion accepts God's generous grace and passes it on to others.

2. PRIESTHOOD

Jesus offers us a true priesthood of all believers. Protestantism
has long affirmed this doctrine but has had difficulty practicing it.
It is a biblical doctrine,[23] but it is too frequently jettisoned in order
for some powerbroker to take advantage of "the system." This

usually means fleecing people of their money and always involves the accumulation of power. The person who claims special status among us by virtue of a call, unique insight, or revelation makes me suspicious. Authoritarian leadership that will not bear accountability, questioning, or challenge is not modeled on Jesus' example.[24]

3. A SUPPORTIVE COMMUNITITY

A church that knows the difference between Christianity and religionism provides a nurturing environment that values and nurtures people while avoiding punitive actions toward them. Religion tends to be dogmatic and judgmental. It promotes an "us-versus-them" mentality. It is meddlesome and intrusive with its members' lives. A society of God that can legitimately call itself a New Testament church is a supportive community where people worship together, pray for one another, and pay attention to one another's needs. Work, education, family, moral choices—all things are viewed in terms of the values embraced and affirmed by the larger body. Without being nosy, members have a sense of responsibility for the welfare of others.

Authentic Christianity defends the weak and reclaims the fallen.[25] When an instance of disfellowship from the group does occur, the supportive community sadly recognizes that love has failed and that one within the group has rejected what was once embraced; this community never punishes, gets even, or protects the group's reputation with onlookers.

4. JOYFUL SERVICE

Genuine Christianity cultivates joy rather than guilt and drudgery in one's service to God. Addictive religion can only talk of its adherents' duties, obligations, and responsibilities. Thus it promotes and rewards workaholic personalities. It demands high-intensity involvement without regard to natural giftedness or personal inclination. And it always leaves a mass of exhausted and burned-out people in its wake.

True religion is very different. While acknowledging the duties of created subjects to their Creator, it does not *begin* there. It offers a true knowledge of God's character and actions that show how utterly desirable God is for his holiness and grace. One who sees this clear vision of God exclaims, "Whom have I in heaven but you? And earth has nothing I desire besides you."[26] One who hears the story of Jesus' redemptive love at Calvary thinks of the Son of God in terms of Bach's "joy of man's desiring" instead of a harsh taskmaster. Seeking to perform one's duties to *this* God or in the name of *this* Jesus could never be a legalistic burden.

Obedience to divine commandments to such a deity only affirms the depth of one's passion for God. In such a setting, people serve in areas where God has gifted them and as God opens the door for their ministries.

5. CHRIST-CENTERED CONFIDENCE

Those who live their faith in a healthy way are reassured by the indwelling Spirit of God and experience a sense of personal well-being, assurance, and peace in their daily lives. In other words, they move from the insecurity and fear of religion addiction to a confidence that is centered in Christ. They no longer live in anxiety but in truth, no longer view eternity in terms of their fear of hell but in hope of heaven. They no longer work to be accepted, but serve in the joy of acceptance by grace.

SYMPTOMS OF RELIGIOUS ADDICTION

Religious addiction does have certain symptoms and stages. The following list can help you identify some of the most obvious signs of religious addiction.

- *Despair.* The addict feels hopeless because his religion is not producing the desired results.

- *Erratic behavior.* Knowing something is wrong and refusing to change his beliefs, the addict attempts to change behavior rather than his heart.

- *Resentment and anger.* As the addict's world falls apart, everyone else is to blame and everyone else is an object of rage.

- *Obsession with beliefs.* Continually wondering what is wrong with her faith, the addict studies through each belief until she is unable to concentrate on anything.

- *Stagnation.* All seems lost to him now, so he obsessively ponders past mistakes.

- *Searching for another fix.* Other addictions such as food, drugs, and sex intensify as the addict seeks relief from other sources.

- *Fear.* The addict seems afraid of everyone because of her insecurity; she is afraid to continue in her toxic faith but is equally afraid to get out.

- *Hitting bottom.* Running out of self-will and manipulation, the religious addict must give up the addiction and turn to God.[27]

Are you wondering whether you might be a religion addict instead of a Christian? In an appendix to Stephen Arterburn and Jack Felton's *Toxic Faith* there is a twenty-point quiz to help people answer that question.[28] I've adapted a few of the questions that can help you decide:

- Do you fear that God will turn his back on you if you do not do enough for him?

- Do you give money to a church or ministry so God will bless you?

- Do you often tell your friends, mate, or children what to do without explaining your reasons, just because you know you are right?

- Do you have to check with your minister or some other trusted interpreter of Scripture in order to decide your "position" on some spiritual issue?
- Do you think you are still being punished by God for something you did a long time ago?
- Do you believe that if you work harder for him, God will eventually forgive you for something you have done?
- Has your religious experience made it hard for you to relate to your family and friends?

An affirmative answer to even one of these questions points to the likelihood that you are an addict to religion, rather than a devotee to the God who has been revealed in Jesus Christ. Multiple positive answers testify to a major problem in your understanding of God—and to great pain in your effort to live for him.

Christ's church does not exist to promote religionism but to announce the gospel of grace. God's people are not on the earth to model religious neuroticism, but to show the world what it is to live in the security of divine acceptance given as an absolutely free gift through Christ.

We are not commissioned to proclaim guilt and holy terror as the incentive for lost people to be saved, for that never stopped anybody from sinning. Instead we are to tell others the story of Christ's love for them that put him on a cross.

Say to him: "Here, Lord, I abandon myself to thee. I have tried in every way I could think of to manage myself, and to make myself what I know I ought to be, but have always failed. Now I give it up to thee. Do thou take entire possession of me. Work in me all the good pleasure of thy will. Mold and fashion me into such a vessel as seemeth good to thee. I leave myself in thy hands, and I believe thou wilt, according to thy promise, make me into a vessel unto thy own honor, 'sanctified, and meet for the master's use, and prepared unto every good work.'" And here you must rest, trusting yourself thus to Him, continually and absolutely.

Hannah Whitall Smith, *The Christian's Secret of a Happy Life*

CHAPTER TWELVE

Commitment

The bulk of this book has concentrated on searching for insights into Jesus' way of handling several of life's negatives. Now a disclaimer must be made so the study can go in a different direction. This disclaimer makes explicit what has been assumed from the start: Jesus could deal with stress, poverty, confusion, and the like because he lived a deeply spiritual life that defined him in terms of his relationship with the Father. Therefore, this chapter will pursue an understanding of the nature of authentic spirituality. While the particular insights of the previous chapters are necessary, they are worthless apart from a total life commitment to God.

The central purpose of this book was made clear in its Introduction: "Disciples seek to understand and emulate [Jesus'] values, his behavior, and his view of reality." So now it is time to glue together the pieces of the world-view that lay beneath the approach to life that our Savior took. We must examine the nature of his personal commitment to God.

Returning once more to the introduction, you may recall the story of Milton Jones's sermon. He challenged the church to be willing to follow Christ anywhere. At the end of that lesson, a recent convert to Christ came to Milton and asked, "Do you mean to tell me that some of the people in this church haven't even decided whether they're going to follow Jesus or not?" It appears that there are people like that in every church. They are still holding out on him and making their life decisions in jigsaw-puzzle fashion. That is, they decide to do what is right here but to compromise there; to follow Jesus' example in this, but not in that. So they are frustrated in their spiritual lives.

If you are still dealing with life that way, you will continue to be frustrated until you give everything over to God. What that means to you and how it will change you is the concern of this chapter.

WHEN DUTY BECOMES DESIRE

The late Batsell Barrett Baxter preached a sermon that he titled "When Duty Becomes Desire." It had a powerful effect on me, because it forced me to admit that my own spiritual life was still only functioning at the level of duty. Not that *duty* is a bad word, you understand. But the service of God must become more than duty to be either meaningful or sustained. That sermon has caused me to think deeply across the years about the nature of spiritual growth.

All the serious personal relationships of our lives have to face the issue of *duty*, i.e., obligations and responsibility. Only in humankind's relationship with God, however, do we tend to begin here. Perhaps this explains why legalism has such a long and fabled legacy across the centuries of church history.

But what if we take another point of departure? What if we thought of our relationship with God on the model of some of the more fundamental bonds we have with significant human beings? While there are limitations and dangers to any attempt to understand our union with God through some argument by analogy, there are also some meaningful insights to be gained.

My own attachment to parents, wife, or children could never be thought of as *duty*. All of them started with *desire*. There was a longing and need within me that reached in the direction of someone else. As those relationships matured, I learned and performed various duties of obedience, nurture, and protection. From these fulfilled obligations has come an undeniable sense of satisfaction and delight.

That some Christians have felt their obedience to God "burdensome"[1] indicates their coming to him was seriously flawed. They were taught to mollify an angry God or to barter with a businesslike God rather than to admire, love, and desire a captivating, winsome God. So they started down the path of obeying commandments with a low motivation—one that eventually degenerated into legalism or simply failed altogether.

Against this world's misdirection of our desire toward designer clothing, bigger houses, or more expensive cars, heaven's directives channel our legitimate desire for God into eager and unforced compliance.

The end of this process is that sense of peaceful delight in God that one knows should come in a true experience of salvation. When your soul has thirsted for God as a deer pants for streams of water,[2] the satisfaction of knowing him and surrendering to him is the ultimate fulfillment.

It is only when we begin with the affirmation of his grace that our hearts are led to desire God, perform our duties out of love, and find delight in the process from start to finish.

How Jesus Lived

An episode from the life of Christ that takes us to the heart of this issue of commitment involves an unnamed character known to us as the Rich Young Ruler. It puts Jesus' concept of the kingdom in contrast with the one most widely held—both in ancient times and today—and makes it clear how complete a believer's life commitment must be.

The Jews of Jesus' day believed that "the present age" would someday give way to "the new age" of the Messiah and his reign, and so they were inclined to ask about salvation in terms of receiving eternal life in the age to come. Thus the man's question: "Good teacher, what must I do to inherit eternal life?"[3] The eventual answer he would receive was this: "Come, follow me." But between the question and the answer come two very important conditions.

Anyone who wants to be part of the kingdom of God and live a life of committed discipleship must first have an obedient heart. That is why Jesus began his response to the young ruler by reminding him of the Ten Commandments. "You know the commandments," Jesus said and reminded him of the laws against murder, adultery, stealing, and the like. "Teacher," he replied, "all these I have kept since I was a boy."

By that response, the young ruler was not claiming to be sinless or that he had never broken any of the commandments of God. He meant that he observed the Law of Moses in good faith and always followed through with repentance and an appropriate sacrifice when he violated a statute. If he had been claiming that he was utterly without fault, Jesus would have responded very differently than he did. The text says: "Jesus looked at him and loved him." That would not have been Jesus' response to a liar's arrogance!

The Son of Man knew that many conscientious lawkeepers were unsure about their salvation and lacked peace of mind. Like this man, they had done their best to keep the commandments but still felt insecure about their prospects for eternal life, salvation, and sharing in the kingdom. Men and women under either of the two great covenants may be dutifully obedient without being saved or feeling good about their spiritual lives.

Thus Jesus moved to the second condition for eternal life, self-denial. Jesus sometimes put his requirement of self-denial in a generic form: "If anyone would come after me, he must deny himself and take up his cross and follow me."[4] To this particular sincere, conscience-driven, and duty-bound man, he put the demand in its bluntest form. Caught up as he was in a lifestyle of wealth, youth, and power, he was told, "Go, sell everything you have and give to the poor, and you will have treasure in heaven. Then come, follow me."

Commentators writing about this story have typically told us that the command to sell everything we own is not a universal requirement of Christianity. And they are correct.[5] But for us to understand that there is no demand on us to forfeit things dear and precious for the sake of Christ would be terribly wrong.

In fact, whatever is dearest and most precious to any one of us is exactly what must be given up for the sake of following Christ. "If anyone comes to me and does not hate his father and mother, his wife and children, his brothers and sisters—yes, even his own life—he cannot be my disciple."[6]

Though one cannot be saved without an obedient heart, obedience to law is not enough to save anyone. Salvation, after all, is by grace rather than through our good work of keeping law. Yet there is no such thing as "cheap grace" in the religion of Jesus Christ. In order to accept the grace of God, you must value God's free gift in Christ more than money, fame, power, family, or life itself. Christ must count for more to you than all of them rolled together, so that you would always choose him over them.

What are you proudest of in your life? Your good family name? A house? Your looks? A car? Your job? Success? Education? Your grandchildren? Whatever there is about you that could make you feel self-satisfied and self-sufficient or better than somebody else is your greatest temptation. It will more likely cost you your soul than some items on a biblical list of vices. It is likely the one thing for which you could be tempted to sacrifice truth, principle, integrity, and Christ.

If you cannot honestly say that your most prized possession, life situation, job, office, or relationship is less important to you than Jesus Christ, your prospect of going to heaven is no greater than the prospect of a camel jumping through the eye of a sewing needle! That's what Jesus told his disciples after the Rich Young Ruler left. "Children," he said, "how hard it is to enter the kingdom of God! It is easier for a camel to go through the eye of a needle than for a rich man to enter the kingdom of God."[7]

Having adopted a lifestyle of obedience to the Word of God and having taken up the cross of denying self for Christ's sake, you are in position to share in the kingdom of God. You can follow Christ in the narrow path that leads to life. You can receive the free gift of eternal life. What was impossible in a lifestyle of disobedience and with an attitude of arrogant self-sufficiency has become possible for you by the grace of God.

Now you are eligible to hear his call to follow him. After all, only those who walk with him can be saved. But to follow Christ is more than getting baptized, being an active church member, and having people think well of you. It is leaving everything else for him.

So the rich man or woman must renounce opulence and indulgence to help the poor and fund the ministry of the gospel. A bright and well-educated person must disown any notion of superiority for the sake of serving in humility. A beautiful woman must repudiate vanity and serve others without patronizing them. Whatever advantage you have must be used for the sake of the kingdom of God, or it will corrupt you, tug your heart away from Jesus, and damn you.

WHAT JESUS TAUGHT

The episode with the Rich Young Ruler ends with Jesus teaching this basic fact about discipleship:

I tell you the truth, no one who has left home or brothers or sisters or mother or father or children or fields for me and the gospel will fail to receive a hundred times as much in this present age (homes, brothers, sisters, mothers, children and fields—and with them, persecutions) and in the age to come, eternal life. But many who are first will be last, and the last first.[8]

Practically all of us understand as much about following Jesus as that wealthy young man did. We know the commands of God, have hearts that want to do right, make a conscientious attempt to follow Scripture, and are penitent when we fail. Yet many of us are also like him in that we are frustrated, insecure, and unsure about eternal life. People like the Rich Young Ruler who know something is lacking must hear the bold words of Jesus about self-denial for the sake of the gospel. That uneasy feeling won't go away until the Master is heard and heeded on this second condition of discipleship.

In his own life, Jesus modeled the commitment to God that he asks of us. He gave up all the rights and prerogatives of deity to come among us as a human being. Can you imagine giving up heaven to live as a peasant in a poor family in an occupied territory? He humbled himself to be tempted in every way we are. Can you fathom a commitment that would cause you to endure all the provocations and indignities he experienced? He died a criminal's death and suffered not only rejection and desertion by men but separation from God as well. Is there any devotion to doing the will of God that could compare with what he exhibited?

Now Jesus asks us to show our commitment to God by selling, walking away from, discounting, or otherwise abandoning all that we are and have for the sake of the kingdom of God. Anything that we might value more than Christ or trust for our security must be given up for Christ. Saul of Tarsus heard that call on his life. Unlike the Rich Young Ruler who walked away in sadness, he gave up everything for Jesus! In his own words:

> Whatever was to my profit I now consider loss for the sake of Christ. What is more, I consider everything a loss compared to the surpassing greatness of knowing Christ Jesus my Lord, for whose sake I have lost all things. I consider them rubbish, that I may gain Christ and be found in him, not having a righteousness of my own that comes from the law, but that which is through faith in Christ—the righteousness that comes from God and is by faith.[9]

Why doesn't everyone follow Paul's example? Carlo Carretto offers one reason for the reluctance.

> Only very late do we learn the price of the risk of believing, because only very late do we face up to the idea of death.
>
> This is what is difficult: believing truly means dying. Dying to everything: to our reasoning, to our plans, to our past, to our childhood dreams, to our attachment to earth, and sometimes even to the sunlight, as at the moment of our physical death.
>
> That is why faith is so difficult. It is so difficult to hear from Jesus a cry of anguish for us in our difficulties in believing, "Oh, if only you could believe!"
>
> Because not even he can take our place in the leap of Faith; it is up to us. It is like dying! It is up to us, and no one is able to take our place. . . .
>
> An act of pure faith is the death of what we love most so it may be offered to the loved one because only love is stronger than death.

FOUR ELEMENTS OF SELF-DENIAL

In order to make the concept of self-denial meaningful, it might help to think of it in terms of four experiences that grow from such a kingdom spirit. Anyone who values commitment to God above all else will exhibit that attitude through personal spiritual disciplines, faith lived in community, compassion, and integrity during times of suffering.

1. SPIRITUAL DISCIPLINES

Ever wish you had the golf game of Lee Trevino or Tiger Woods? Did you ever wonder how you would feel if you drilled the championship basket at the NCAAs? Or maybe you've watched a movie and envisioned yourself in the starring role. Most of us have entertained such fantasies at one time or another.

You've probably done the same thing in your spiritual life. Ever see someone walk away from an attempted seduction by drugs, sex, or money and wonder what you would do in the same situation? Ever tell a friend you wish you had the prayer life or Bible knowledge of some mature Christian you know? Or maybe you're worrying about how to deal with financial problems or growing old and dying.

When we watch star athletes or mature Christians function, we sometimes forget what lies behind the little glimpse we get. The golfer who sinks the $800,000 putt has spent thousands of hours on a putting green to get his stroke right. The actress on screen has trained for years, tediously memorized every line, and rehearsed endlessly. The big moment doesn't come without the tedium of daily work at one's craft.

Maturity in spiritual life is no different. Jesus could quote Scripture to Satan in the wilderness temptation because he lived with it in regular synagogue study and personal meditation. He could forgive the taunting mob on the day of his crucifixion because he dealt graciously with people every day.

Skilled surgeons, superstar athletes, and faithful disciples have the same thing in common: *personal discipline in their fields of expertise.* They could not do the spectacular things without sometimes-tedious practice. The extra hours of devotion to behind-the-scenes, nonglamorous training makes them excel when others fade.

If you want your faith to endure the test, you have to train. Your daily exercise in Bible reading, prayer, and waiting before God prepares you for a crisis. Don't be surprised if you collapse on the course if you are not training daily.

If you want to model Christ's holiness to your children or coworkers, you have to discipline yourself in the "little things" of truthfulness, pure speech, and respectful treatment of others. These are the daily habits that give you strength for the great test you will face someday.

What you do when put "on the spot" in public view is most often what has become second nature to you when you are not in the spotlight. Crisis, opportunity, or persecution simply brings into the full view of others what is habitual for you. So if you've ever wondered what people mean when they talk about spiritual disciplines and if you've been curious about the difference they might make in your life, now you know. But these are the daily personal habits of people whose hearts are committed to God. These people know God in private and seek his heart with the desire of a deer panting for water in the desert.

2. FAITH LIVED IN COMMUNITY

These same people also know, however, that salvation is not a one-on-one experience with God. It is lived in community. The church is the place where people committed to God show that they understand commitment to one another.

Occasionally we human beings sense a light going on in our heads. We refer to what happens in those moments as insight or discovery. Sometimes we even flatter ourselves as having had a "moment of brilliance." A panel of scientists held a conference in Washington in 1996 to share their findings on an important matter. The conference carried the impressive title "The Integrative Neurobiology of Affiliation." Their "findings" boiled down to this: *People need one another.*

What some people are just now stumbling onto is what Jesus told us from the start. People need each other in order to live out their commitment to God. They need encouragement, support, and challenge for the sake of their kingdom ambitions.

Children who are not held, played with, and otherwise loved have a significantly greater likelihood of growing up as disturbed and dangerous people. Psychologists who have studied the frightening rise in violent crime (i.e., mugging, rape, random violence) among teens point to the consistent absence of intact families with nurturing adults. In particular, males growing up without a father to model and teach basic life skills to them tend to do poorly in school and have a high incidence of trouble with the law.

Adults who isolate themselves from the world around them are prone to die much younger than those who cultivate companionship. Theodore J. Kaczynski, the man the FBI believes is the Unabomber, may well become the classic case study of how isolationists are inclined to anger and paranoia; they may not only reject and flee authority but also attack it without remorse.

Disorders such as autism and schizophrenia make it impossible for people to connect with or love others. But there is unambiguous evidence that people without these unchosen problems lose their mental health as a result of choosing to withdraw from others. Even those people who have a good reason for electing solitude (e.g., monks, arctic researchers) are not always unharmed by it; some repudiate their isolation to rejoin a larger community, and others remain secluded only to lose their emotional balance or sanity.

The God who created us has always known and tried to help us understand that he made us to be social creatures. He sets us in families, inclines us to create villages and cities, and places those he saves in a spiritual community called the church. Salvation is not a correspondence course between each believer and God. It is an experience to be lived out within social settings.

The fact that some sisters and brothers are difficult to know, love, or work with simply proves that community is challenging, not that it is unnecessary. Some relationships are easier and more natural than others. The way we choose to live within community tells a great deal about our relationship with God. It exposes any false claim we have made to self-denial for the sake of God and the brothers and sisters he has given us.

"If anyone says, 'I love God,' yet hates his brother, he is a liar. For anyone who does not love his brother, whom he has seen, cannot love God, whom he has not seen. And he has given us this command: Whoever loves God must also love his brother."[10]

3. COMPASSION

To know God is to share his concern for helping the neediest, weakest, and most defenseless. It is to take care of sick children, address the needs of people in prison, or put clothes on the backs of people burned out of their homes. Jesus said that anyone doing such things will be counted as having done them to him personally when he returns to judge the world.[11]

Stories of personal generosity touch most of us—especially accounts of sacrificial kindness concerning people who have very limited resources themselves. A little boy in Nashville whose family had been burned out of their apartment gave one of the two suits of clothing someone provided him to a friend in the same complex who still had only the clothes on his back.

Going to church, reading the Bible, and praying are good. But they are empty efforts until they move us "to know God" by the lifestyles we adopt in this world. James C. Fehnagen, in *Mutual Ministry*, brings our responsibility to those who suffer into sharp focus:

> When Paul talks about "suffering with those who suffer," he is talking about compassion, that supreme gift without which we are less than fully human. It might well be that the greatest threat to human survival now confronting us is not the loss of energy or the increase of pollution, but the loss of compassion.
>
> We are confronted daily with the pain of human tragedy—the breakup of a family or the sunken face of a

starving child—to such an extent that we soon learn to turn off what we see. In order to cope with our feelings of helplessness, we teach ourselves how not to feel. The tragedy in this response, which is probably more widespread than we dare believe, is that we also deaden our capacity for love.

For Christians, the cross stands as an ever-present reminder that love and suffering are two sides of the same coin.

Compassion is a practical and essential element to self-denial, for it means that we have learned to value others and be unselfish with things under our control.

4. INTEGRITY IN SUFFERING

The final element necessary to self-denial is suffering for Jesus' sake. Just go back to what the Lord told his disciples after the wealthy ruler had left. He assured them that those who gave up all for his sake would receive eternal life in the age to come and "homes, brothers, sisters, mothers, children and fields—and with them persecutions" in the present age. As much as we would like to make suffering an optional component to commitment and faithfulness, Jesus identified it as an essential feature of discipleship.

You've read the stories and seen the live television coverage of the raging fires that periodically hit California. Thousands and thousands of acres may be scorched. Houses get burned to the ground. It is scary to watch—even from the safe distance of a television news report.

But do you realize that these same destructive fires are also incredibly creative? More than that, they are even necessary to keeping the land alive and productive.

Fire can process dead material in forests into nutrients more quickly than decay. Many pine cones require temperatures of one hundred and twenty degrees or higher to burst open so they can distribute their seeds and create new trees. Some species of birds thrive only in areas regularly burned. Quail, for example, need burned-over areas so the undergrowth will not get too thick and overgrown for them.

Spiritual life is amazingly similar to those fires. Trial is necessary to purify faith and open doors of growth. Don't all of us tend to complain—maybe even whine—about the problems, unexpected challenges, and unfair features of our lives? Maybe complaints similar to the following have escaped your lips:

- "It shouldn't be so hard to live an upright life! God shouldn't let Satan tempt us with his wiles and threaten us with his evil powers."

- "There are just too many demands," says a high school student. "You can't fit in with some people if you live by Christian standards. They make fun of you. I shouldn't have to go through something like that."

- "Just when I thought I had it made," an older person says, "here comes a heart problem I'll have to deal with for the rest of my life. It just doesn't seem fair that God lets things like this happen to his children!"

When you are inclined to think life isn't fair, I challenge you to realize that life works just the way it should. Challenges produce character. Difficulties evoke creativity and compassion. Life's trials make us realize our need for God. Your willingness to deal with these pressures, temptations, and limitations is nothing more or less than self-denial on a daily basis. The Bible says: "These [trials] have come so that your faith—of greater worth than gold, which perishes even though refined by fire—may be proved genuine and may result in praise, glory and honor when Jesus Christ is revealed."[12]

Jesus gave up heaven so you and I could be saved. The Rich Young Ruler couldn't give up his wealth for eternal life. Abraham was willing to slay his precious Isaac for the sake of his faith in God. Paul discarded everything he had ever deemed valuable for the sake of following Christ. Judas couldn't give up his dream of a militaristic deliverer for Jesus as Messiah. Noah, Sarah, Joseph, Rahab, Samuel, David—the list goes on and on, and somewhere on that list is your name.

Does heaven mean more to you than earth? Is truth more precious than self-deception? Do you love God more than self, Christ more than anything? These are the questions that hold eternity in the balance for all of us.

NOTES

INTRODUCTION

1. John 13:13–16.

2. Scott Peck, *Further Along the Road Less Traveled* (New York: Simon and Schuster, 1993), p. 210.

3. Dallas Willard, *The Spirit of the Disciplines* (San Francisco: Harper & Row, 1988), p. 9. Emphasis added.

4. Luke 9:57–62; cf. Luke 14:25–33.

5. Mark 8:17–18, 21.

6. Oliver Sacks, *An Anthropologist on Mars* (New York: Alfred A. Knopf, 1995), pp. 141–42.

7. Leonard I. Sweet, "Magna Charta of Trust," *Sweet's SoulCafe*, 2 (March 1996), pp. 6–7.

CHAPTER 1. THE WORLD

1. Matt. 5:13–16, emphasis added.

2. Matt. 5:3–12.

3. Matt. 5:16.

4. Matt. 5:20.

5. John 17:18.

6. Heb. 4:15.

7. Luke 7:34.

8. Luke 7:36–39.

9. In Luke's account of the temptation, he points out that "for forty days he was tempted by the devil" (Luke 4:2).

10. Luke 4:13.

11. Heb. 4:15.

12. Heb. 11:13–14.

13. 1 Pet. 2:11–12.

14. Phil. 3:20.

15. 1 John 2:15–17.

16. 1 Cor. 5:9–10.

17. Of course, Vanauken also punched hypocritical Christianity in the nose: "But the strongest argument against Christianity is also Christians—when they are somber and joyless, when they are self-righteous and smug in complacent consecration, when they are narrow and repressive, then Christianity dies a thousand deaths."

CHAPTER 2. SEXUALITY

1. Matt. 19:4.

2. Matt. 5:27–30.

3. Matt. 15:19–20.

4. 1 John 4:2–3.

5. Heb. 4:15.

6. John 4:4–26.

7. John 8:1–11.

8. Luke 7:36–50.

9. Leigh Montville, "Trials of David," *Sports Illustrated* (April 29, 1996), p. 92.

CHAPTER 3. STRESS

1. "The Boorda Tragedy," *USA Today* (May 20, 1996), p. 12A.

2. John Marks, "Time Out," *U.S. News & World Report* (Dec. 11, 1995), p. 88.

3. Barbara Bailey Reinhold, "Toxic Work" as reported in *USA Today* (June 4, 1996), p. 4d.

4. Matt. 2:16 ff.

5. John 7:1–5.

6. Matt. 4:1 ff.

7. 1 Cor. 10:13.

8. Matt. 6:25–34.

9. Myron S. Augsburger, *Matthew* (Waco, Tex.: Word Books, 1982), p. 94. Adapted from the book.

10. Meyer Friedman, M.D., Ray Rosenman, M.D., *Type A Behavior and Your Heart* (n.p., n.d.).

11. Ps. 46:1; cf. Eph. 6:10 ff.

12. 2 Cor. 12:10.

13. 1 Pet. 5:7.

14. 1 Tim. 6:6, 8.

15. Cf. James 2:8 ff.; 1 John 3:16 ff.; Gal. 6:2.

16. Prov. 17:22.

17. Cf. Acts 16:6–8.

18. 2 Tim. 1:7.

19. John 16:33.

CHAPTER 4. MONEY

1. Richard Leider, *Repacking Your Bags: Lighten Your Load for the Rest of Your Life* (n.p., nd.).

2. Laurence Shames, *The Hunger for More* (New York: Times Books, 1989).

3. Luke 6:20, 24; Matt. 6:19; 19:21, 23; Luke 12:15.

4. Matt. 6:19–21, 24.

5. Luke 12:15.

6. Matt. 6:33.

7. Matt. 16:26.

8. Luke 16:8.

9. Luke 16:10–12.

10. Ps. 24:1.

11. Luke 16:19 ff.

12. Luke 9:58.

13. Matt. 6:11; Luke 8:3.

14. John 14:26.

15. John 14:27.

16. John 15:13.

17. John 17:3.

18. John 14:1–4.

19. John 17:24.

20. 2 Cor. 8:9.

21. Willard, *Spirit of the Disciplines,* p. 194.

22. Phil. 4:11b–13.

23. Phil. 1:21.

CHAPTER 5. COMPETITION

1. *U.S. News & World Report,* March 4, 1996, p. 29.

2. John 7:3–4.

3. John 7:5.

4. Luke 12:13.

5. Mark 9:38.

6. Luke 8:19–21.

7. Cf. 1 Cor. 6:1–8.

8. Luke 12:21.

9. Maureen Dowd, "Ted's Excellent Idea," *New York Times,* August 22, 1996.

10. Mark 9:39–40.

11. Matt. 18:1–4.

12. Cf. Matt. 7:12.

13. William Barclay, *Flesh and Spirit* (Nashville: Abingdon Press, 1962), p. 44.

CHAPTER 6. HONESTY

1. Stephen L. Carter, "Becoming People of Integrity," *Christian Century*, March 13, 1996.

2. James Patterson and Peter Kim, *The Day America Told the Truth* (New York: Prentice Hall Press, 1991), p. 45.

3. Luke 2:49; John 18:37.

4. John 18:37.

5. John 8:44–47.

6. See, e.g., John 5:19, 24, 25; 6:26, 32, 53. The phrase "I tell you the truth" in these and other passages is a translation of the word *amen*, which he uses twice each time for emphasis. Older translations read, "Verily, verily I tell you. . . ."

7. John 17:17.

8. John 14:17.

9. John 7:12. Just after this, Jesus pointed to one sign of his truthfulness: that he was bringing glory and honor to God rather than to himself. "My teaching is not my own. It comes from him who sent me. If any one chooses to do God's will, he will find out whether my teaching comes from God or whether I speak on my own. He who speaks on his own does so to gain honor for himself, but he who works for the honor of the one who sent him is a man of truth; there is nothing false about him" (John 7:16–18).

10. John 8:31 ff; cf. John 14:6.

11. John 1:17.

CHAPTER 7. INJUSTICE

1. Deut. 19:21; cf. Exod. 21:22–25; Lev. 24:19–20.

2. Matt. 5:39–42.

3. Matt. 5:43–48.

4. Lev. 19:18.

5. Frederick Buechner, *The Magnificent Defeat* (San Francisco: Harper & Row, 1966), p. 105.

6. Matt. 18:21 ff.

7. Matt. 18:23–34.

8. Eph. 4:32.

9. Matt. 6:12.

10. Luke 9:51–55.

11. Isa. 53:4–5.

12. Luke 23:34.

13. 1 Pet. 2:21–23.

14. Luke 22:31–32. cf. John 21:15–19.

15. Lewis Smedes, "Forgiveness: the Power to Change the Past," *Christianity Today*, Jan. 7, 1983, p. 26.

CHAPTER 8. DEATH

1. John Updike, *Rabbit at Rest* (New York: Alfred A. Knopf, 1990), p. 176.

2. John Bunyan, *The Pilgrim's Progress* (Westwood, NJ: Barbour and Company, Inc., n.d.).

3. Heb. 2:14–15.

4. Mark 8:31–37.

5. Juan Carlos Ortiz, *Disciple* (Altamonte Springs, Fla.: Creation House), p. 31.

6. Matt. 10:28.

7. John 14:1–4.

8. John 12:23–25.

9. Luke 7:22.

10. Diane Komp, *Hope Springs from Mended Places* (San Francisco: Harper, 1994), pp. 72–82.

11. See Mark 5:21–43.

12. Luke 7:11–17.

13. John 11:21–24.

14. John 1:4; 17:3.

15. Rom. 8:38–39.

16. See 1 Cor. 15:55.

17. Bunyan, *Pilgrim's Progress*.

18. Phil. 1:21, 23.

CHAPTER 9. POVERTY

1. "The Coin and the Spirit," review of *God and Mammon in America* by Robert Wuthrow, *Time* (Sept. 26, 1994, p.82).
2. Jer. 22:13–17, emphasis added.
3. Luke 21:4.
4. Luke 2:7.
5. Luke 1:48.
6. Luke 1:52–53.
7. Luke 2:24.
8. Lev. 12:6–8.
9. Luke 3:11.
10. Luke 9:58.
11. Luke 6:1–5; cf. Deut. 23:25.
12. Matt. 17:24–27.
13. Luke 8:1–3.
14. Luke 4:16 ff.
15. Lev. 25:11 ff.
16. Matt. 26:11.
17. Luke 10:25–37.
18. Luke 12:13–21.
19. Luke 16:11–13.
20. 1 John 3:17–18.
21. Richard J. Foster, *The Freedom of Simplicity* (New York: Harper & Row, 1981) p. 142.
22. Acts 2:45.
23. Acts 4:32.
24. Peter Marshall, *The Prayers of Peter Marshall* (New York: McGraw Hill Book Co., 1954).
25. 1 Tim. 6:10.
26. 1 Tim. 6:17–19.

CHAPTER 10. CONFUSION

1. Luke 6:12–13.
2. Luke 22:40–44.

3. John 4:34.

4. Eccles. 12:13–14.

5. 1 John 4:20.

6. John 8:1–11.

7. Lev. 20:10.

8. Exod. 23:1; cf. Deut. 19:16 ff.

9. Luke 13:10 ff.; cf. Matt. 12:1 ff.

10. Mark 2:27.

11. Gen. 16:2.

12. Gen. 16:4.

13. Gen. 16:5–6.

14. Gen. 16:8.

15. Gen. 16:9.

16. Gen. 16:13–14.

17. 2 Cor. 12:7–10.

18. Gen. 37:2–41:46.

19. Rom. 8:28.

20. Henri Nouwen, "A Desperate Prayer," *A Cry for Mercy* (n.p.: Orbis Books, 1994).

21. Matt. 26:41.

22. Harry Emerson Fosdick, *The Meaning of Prayer.*

23. Luke 22:43.

CHAPTER 11. RELIGION

1. 2 Chron. 30:18.

2. 2 Chron. 30:18–20.

3. Amos 5:21–23.

4. Amos 5:24.

5. Isa. 1:14–17.

6. Cf. James 1:27.

7. Joseph F. Girzone, *Joshua: A Parable for Today* (New York: Macmillan Publishing Co., 1983), pp. 73–75.

8. Luke 13:10–14.

9. Luke 13:15–16.

10. Mark 7:3–4.

11. Mark 7:5–10.

12. Matt. 23:13–14 *THE MESSAGE.*

13. Matt. 23:11 *THE MESSAGE.*

14. Matt. 23:15 *THE MESSAGE.*

15. Matt. 23:16–22 *THE MESSAGE.*

16. Christian Smith, "Is the Church Interested in the Kingdom?" *Voices,* July/August 1989, pp. 2–5.

17. Matt. 23:23–24 *THE MESSAGE.*

18. Matt. 23:25–26 *THE MESSAGE.*

19. John 8:34.

20. Rom. 8:6–8.

21. Phil. 3:2–6.

22. Phil. 3:8.

23. 1 Pet. 2:9.

24. Cf. Mark 10:42–45.

25. John 8:1–11.

26. Ps. 73:25.

27. Stephen Arterburn, Jack Felton, *Toxic Faith* (Nashville: Thomas Nelson Publishers, 1991).

28. Ibid.

CHAPTER 12. COMMITMENT

1. Cf. 1 John 5:3.

2. Ps. 42:1–2.

3. Mark 10:17 ff.

4. Matt. 16:24.

5. Cf. Acts 5:4.

6. Luke 14:26.

7. Mark 10:24–25.

8. Mark 10:29–31.

9. Phil. 3:7–9.

10. 1 John 4:19–21.

11. Matt. 25:34–40.

12. 1 Pet. 1:7.

Printed in the United States
By Bookmasters